Get the
INTERVIEW EDGE!

Get the
INTERVIEW EDGE!

TIPS to Getting Hired
from *INTERVIEWERS*

KIM CHUNG AND **ELISA HUI**

To order direct from the author please contact Kim Chung and Elisa Hui
email: gethirednow@gmail.com
www.gettingyouhired.com

Note for Librarians: a cataloguing record for this book that includes Dewey Decimal Classification and US Library of Congress numbers is available from the Library and Archives of Canada. The complete cataloguing record can be obtained from their online database at:
www.collectionscanada.ca/amicus/index-e.html
ISBN 1-4120-3928-2

TRAFFORD

Offices in Canada, USA, Ireland, UK and Spain
This book was published on-demand in cooperation with Trafford Publishing. On-demand publishing is a unique process and service of making a book available for retail sale to the public taking advantage of on-demand manufacturing and Internet marketing. On-demand publishing includes promotions, retail sales, manufacturing, order fulfilment, accounting and collecting royalties on behalf of the author.
Book sales for North America and international:
Trafford Publishing, 6E–2333 Government St.,
Victoria, BC v8т 4p4 CANADA
phone 250 383 6864 (toll-free 1 888 232 4444)
fax 250 383 6804; email to orders@trafford.com
Book sales in Europe:
Trafford Publishing (uk) Ltd., Enterprise House, Wistaston Road Business Centre,
Wistaston Road, Crewe, Cheshire cw2 7rp UNITED KINGDOM
phone 01270 251 396 (local rate 0845 230 9601)
facsimile 01270 254 983; orders.uk@trafford.com
Order online at:
www.trafford.com/robots/04-1736.html

10 9 8 7 6 5 4 3 2 1

TABLE OF CONTENTS

Get the
INTERVIEW EDGE!

TIPS to Getting Hired

from *INTERVIEWERS*

FOREWORD

Dear Job Seeker,

Today, getting a job is becoming harder and harder. Organizations may receive as many as 500 applications for every one job opening they have. That's like having a job offered to only the top 0.2% of applicants! Talk about only taking the cream of the crop! So even if you think you are in the top 10%, or top 1%, you will still have a lot of strong competition to face! In fact, it takes on average 12 interviews to get one job offer. The statistics alone explain why looking for a job could be such a demotivating experience and why the job search process is difficult for everyone!

Your time is precious. Wouldn't it be frustrating if the book you chose only wasted your time because it told you things you already knew? Or worse yet, you are told to memorize 100 different questions and answers that don't even get asked in your interview?

Fortunately, this book is different. It can help increase your chances of landing the job you want by improving your overall interview skills! You will learn a *formula* for answering the two key styles of interview questions: *holistic* and *behavioural* — which will then enable you to do well in almost any interview — when faced with almost any question! You will learn to:

- ▸ structure your responses to maximize impact
- ▸ distinguish between weak, strong and exceptional answers to behavioral questions
- ▸ anticipate questions
- ▸ ask the right questions in return
- ▸ avoid mistakes most candidates make

Reading this book, you *will* have an unfair advantage over other applicants!

The examples in this book were written with recent graduating students (undergraduates or graduates) in mind. Although many of the examples provided are very relevant to recent graduates, the tips, competency definitions and scale descriptions, are relevant to all who seek a job.

This book was written by two experienced interviewers to help you get the job you want! We know what interviewers are looking for because we have interviewed candidates as part of our jobs! We gladly share our combined recruiting experiences with you in hopes that you will receive many job offers. We believe that the more insider knowledge you have combined with sound interviewing strategies, the greater your chances for success in landing the job you want!

All the best in your job search!

Kim Chung & Elisa Hui

Introduction
— How we'll help you succed

We are different from other interview books because we will:

▶ teach you a technique to deliver powerful answers

▶ help you understand what each skill means by *defining* each *competency*

▶ give you sample *questions* corresponding to each competency

▶ provide you with examples of weak, strong and exceptional *answers*

▶ analyze answers so you know why they are or are not exceptional

▶ provide quick tips on how to make your answers *stronger*

▶ provide practical advice to *avoid the mistakes* most candidates make

What we will not do:

▶ have you memorize 101 most common interview questions and answers

▶ waste your time by giving you information you probably already know (e.g. give a firm handshake, dress business formal for an interview etc.)

To succeed in an interview, you need to know three things:

1. Know what the interviewer wants

2. Have a technique to deliver a strong and consistent image

3. Believe in yourself!

1. *Know what the interview wants:*

   The interviewer seeks to:

   ▸ determine if you have the skills to do the job well (their needs)

   ▸ determine if you could take the job to a new level of effectiveness (their desires)

   ▸ uncover red flags that may signal potential performance problems (their fears)

   This book gives you the tools to anticipate what these needs/desires/fears are. *The questions many interviewers ask can be grouped as **behavioural** and **holistic**.* To answer behavioural questions effectively you need to understand how skills are defined so you can best meet the interviewers most basic needs. To answer holistic questions effectively you need to know the rationale for a question and the various danger signals interviewers are looking for. Throughout this book, we help you understand how interviewers assess responses to the 12 most common behavioural and 11 most common holistic questions.

2. *Have a technique to deliver a strong and consistent image*

   To convince the interviewer you are the best, you need to deliver a strong and consistent message. You need to know how to structure your responses succinctly and clearly. We will teach you how to do this with a technique called **BAR** *(Background, Action, Results).*

3. *Believe in yourself!*

   Finally, you need to have confidence and believe you are the best person for the job. By the end of this book, after you have learned all the techniques and tips we are about to teach you — you will have a strong advantage over other candidates — so you will have the right to be confident!

   Let's get started!

Holistic & Behavioural _INTERVIEWS:_

An overview of the two key styles of questions:

Two key styles of questioning can be referred to as behavioural and holistic.

 **Behavioural Questions:**

Behavioural Interviews ask questions related to competencies. Competencies are skills, abilities, behaviours or personal characteristics that lead to successful job performance. Many organizations believe past performance is an indicator of future success. In behavioural interviews, the interviewer will ask you about how you behaved in the past to determine your likelihood of success on the job in the future. The questions usually come in the form of: "Tell me about a time when you've demonstrated strong "x" skills".

Behavioural interviews aim to determine:
- whether you have the necessary *competency* for the job
- your proficiency *level* per competency

Where will you fall on the scale?
Each competency has different levels of proficiencies typically described in the form of a scale. The scale could have 3, 4, or 5 different grades, which range from "weak" to "exceptional" and is used to rate your answers.

A **weak score** usually means the candidate:
- *does not exhibit* the competency or only meets the *minimal behavioural requirements*
- *appears uncomfortable* exhibiting the competency
- *hinders* or does not achieve results

A **strong score** usually means the candidate:
- has a very good *grasp* of this skill
- knows *when* and *how* to use it
- achieves strong results

An **exceptional score** usually means the candidate not only demonstrates the strong behaviours proficiently but also:
- helps *others* harness this skill
- *customizes* the use of the skill to specific situations
- *proactively* anticipates and removes barriers and/or
- achieves *breakthrough* results

How we will help you:

Many organizations have a customized set of competencies for each of their jobs. Although competencies are usually defined differently by organizations because of their business needs, there are some key underlying similarities. Understanding competencies and their proficiency levels will help you understand what interviewers are looking for. To help you, we have researched and defined the 12 most sought after competencies many interviewers look for. These competencies are defined in a 3-point scale that mimics how interviewers may rate your interview performance.

Here is a list of the competencies we will cover in the "Interview Questions & Answers" section of the book. Instead of trying to remember the 100 most common interview questions, YOU ONLY NEED TO REMEMBER 12!

List of 12 Competencies

▸ Leadership	▸ Analytical Thinking	▸ Communication
▸ Risk-Taking	▸ Creative Thinking	▸ Results-Oriented
▸ Teamwork	▸ Ethics	▸ Learning
▸ Time Management	▸ Initiative	▸ Flexibility

 **INTERVIEW TIP**

Many organizations have competency-based performance evaluation systems to rate their existing employees' performance. It is likely these same organizations use these same competencies to evaluate job applicants. Consider asking someone you know who is working in the organization or the interviewer for a copy of the competency-based performance evaluation for the job you are applying to. This would give you an idea about how you could be rated in the interview.

 # Holistic Questions:

In addition to assessing whether you qualify for the job (with behavioural questions), the interviewer also determines whether you would be a good fit for the position and organization. This is where holistic questions come in. Holistic questions try to understand:

▸ your *underlying motivation* and *intentions*
▸ *who* you are
▸ *why* you are applying to the job

These questions help the interviewer understand whether you would truly be happy in the position because if you are, this would likely reflect positively on your job performance.

Respond with an Edge

Unlike behavioural questions, holistic questions are usually not rated on a scale. Instead, the interviewer will decide if the answer is typical or gives you an edge above other candidates. A typical answer is not a good answer because it will not help you stand out as the person that should be hired. Responses with an edge make you memorable and reinforce to the interviewer that you are a good fit for the position.

How we will help you:

When asking holistic questions, the interviewer is searching for certain qualities. Sometimes, the qualities are easy to identify (i.e. positive attitude, easy to get along with, etc) and other times they are not (i.e. reasoning for your least favourite job experience, your five year goal, etc). We will give you specific qualities interviewers are looking for so you will be prepared to deliver answers that give you an edge above others!

Here is a list of the 11 most common types of holistic questions which we will go through in more detail under the "Interview Questions & Answers" section:

11 Most Common Types of Holistic Questions

▸ Résumé

▸ Interest

▸ Fit

▸ Strengths/Weaknesses

▸ Work Pattern

▸ Well Roundedness

▸ Drive

▸ Attitude

▸ Watch Outs

▸ Long Term Goals

▸ Hypothetical/Case Study

Now that you are aware of the two key methods of interview questioning, we will teach how to deliver strong answers. The technique to learn is **BAR** *(Background, Action, Results).*

BAR (Background, Action, Results)

— The technique to delivering strong answers!

BAR
(Background, Action, Results)

BAR is a method of structuring your responses to create impact. It's an acronym for: Background, Action, Results. It is designed to help the interviewer understand why you are so amazing. **To do this, the most important component to get right is the first part: The Background.**

▶ The Background

The *background* provides context. It sets the stage for you to share your experiences. To positively stand out in the eyes of the interviewers, there are several things you could do:

1. Describe the background in the context of an obstacle that you overcame so that the interviewer will appreciate the value of your work.

2. Describe *why* the situation seemed insurmountable.

3. Know how you will be describing your actions in advance. This will help determine the key details you will require to explain the relevancy of your actions

4. Provide essential information in your description of the back ground. For example, if you are answering an analytical question, don't just say you did an analysis; instead outline the various types of data you had to sort through. This will help interviewer appreciate the complexity of your work. Just don't bore the interviewer with too much detail!

5. Offer a *unique* situation. Some interviewers have seen hundreds of candidates and a common situation won't make you exceptional. You want to be remembered, not forgotten.

6. Choose an example where you noticed an opportunity for improvement.

▶ INTERVIEW TIP

*Words like **however, but, unfortunately**, can help outline an obstacle, and demonstrate the uniqueness of a background*

▶ The Action

After building the context, describe your actions. You have to help the interviewer understand how the action you took in the past was done *better than how anyone else* had or could have done it. That is how you will distinguish yourself. Some key points to remember are:

1. Use the word "I" — not "we"

2. Describe how you *overcame* an obstacle.

3. Reveal the *reasoning* for your actions. *Why* did you do that? Give the interviewer insight into the *way* you *think*.

4. Describe your actions in chronological order, this makes it easier for the interviewer to follow you.

5. Demonstrate *structured* thoughts in your action steps. Don't just ramble — segment your reasoning/logic into buckets — *categorize* the different alternatives you thought through so that it's easy for the interviewer to follow. For example, if you had 3 alternatives, say that up front and quickly capture how they are different.

6. Use the definition and key words contained in the job description to describe your actions.

7. Briefly explain the consequences if you *didn't* do what you did.

8. Describe why your action was *better than how anyone else* had or could have done it.

INTERVIEW TIP

Even if you are describing a team effort — remember to use "I" as well as "we" in your sentences. The interviewer is considering hiring YOU — not your team or any other group of people. Even if you were part of a team — YOU still had YOUR thoughts — YOU still had YOUR actions — YOUR initiatives! When an interviewer hears "we" it may discredit the candidate. The interviewer may think many other people took leads or initiatives and you just benefited from the ride.

▶ The Results

Now that you've told your interviewer what you did, tell him what the end results of those actions were. This is where you would answer the "so what?" to everything you've just been talking about. Some tips while doing this:

1. Use data when possible to give credibility — exact numbers would be ideal.

2. Describe what *changes* occurred because of your actions. What was the *impact*?

3. Outline what you *achieved*.

4. If you *exceeded* the goals, say so! Then strengthen it by saying by how much.

5. Describe how your results were better than others.

<u>So remember</u> **BAR!** Use this structure for every question. You must also practice delivering your answers out loud. Check that you've described each part of BAR and that it flows naturally. This method is easy to apply and it will strengthen your answers. To make your answer even more effective, we will now show you how to use **BAR** in slightly different ways to create bigger impact depending on the type of question you get asked.

 # BAR FOR BEHAVIOURAL TIP

Remember three tips:

1. *Build a strong background.*
2. *Make sure your answer is easy to follow.*
3. *Integrate the definition of "exceptional" for the competency in your answer.*

BAR for Behavioural Questions:

1. Build a strong background

Behavioural questions ask you to give examples from your past. Understand that the interviewer is not familiar with what happened, so ensure that you disclose all relevant information. Take the time to build a strong background. Since, competencies are key to the interviewer, he will be willing to spend the time to understand your answers.

2. Make sure your answer is easy to follow

Understand the interviewer may not be familiar with what you may consider to be basic information. Most organizations who use behavioural interviews value the way a candidate thinks more than the discipline which the candidate studied. As such, an interviewer who majored in psychology could be interviewing a candidate who is studying engineering to become a Marketing Manager. Use layman's terms and avoid technical descriptions. Give structured answers so you don't sound like your mind is jumping all over the place. If you are going to take your interviewer through three different alternatives you had to think through, say so. Don't just say, "and *then* I thought…and then I thought…" If the interviewer is confused, he won't fully appreciate your answer.

3. Integrate the definition of "exceptional" for the competency

You are going to learn the qualities that make a candidate exceptional. Incorporate these qualities (the name of it, the definition of it) into your answers. The easier you make it for the interviewer to understand that you are exceptional, the likelier it is that he will rate you as such.

Examples of how to apply these tips are in the "Interview Questions & Answers — Behavioural" section of this book.

BAR FOR HOLISTIC TIP

Remember three tips:

1. Convert question into a behavioural question
2. Choose competency carefully
3. Keep it short

BAR for Holistic Questions:

1. Convert question into a behavioural question

Holistic questions are used to understand who you are and your underlying intentions. Often times, this part of the interview sometimes feels more like a chat, appearing easier to answer than behavioural questions. Don't be fooled. This is where the majority of candidates give typical answers that do not help the interviewer to truly understand their fit for the job. When this is unclear, a job offer will not likely follow. Since most candidates do not fully prepare for this part and end up giving typical answers, this is your chance to stand out and use holistic questions to encourage the interviewer to hire you.

To stand out you need to put in as much effort in answering holistic questions as you would behavioural questions. *Give the unexpected by converting the holistic question into a behavioural answer.* The interviewer is not asking for a competency directly but he will always be looking for evidence of it throughout the interview. Make the transition subtle and brief. Provide an example in your response, which also *happens* to demonstrate a competency.

2. Choose the competency carefully

When doing this, you must *choose the competency carefully*. Holistic questions typically do not target a specific competency and therefore you have a choice about which competency you would like to emphasize. Choose one that either strengthens your example, or is one that you know the interviewer particularly values for this position.

3. Keep it short

Finally, *keep it short*! Holistic questions are not used to assess your qualifications; they act more as a source of reassurance for the recruiter. Therefore, this is not the area of focus for the interviewer. Translation — do NOT take up too much time answering these questions.

Examples of how these tips are applied are in the "Interview Questions & Answers - Holistic" section of this book.

Interview Questions & Answers

BEHAVIOURAL

Interview Questions & Answers — Behavioural

Using the BAR technique for behavioural and holistic questions is simple and effective! Now let's put all of your learning to practice! Below, is the list of 12 key competencies many organizations ask about:

List of 12 Competencies

▸ Leadership	▸ Analytical Thinking	▸ Communication
▸ Risk-Taking	▸ Creative Thinking	▸ Results-Oriented
▸ Teamwork	▸ Ethics	▸ Learning
▸ Time Management	▸ Initiative	▸ Flexibility

For each competency we will give you:

1. the definition

2. the weak, strong and exceptional description

3. examples of how each competency question could be asked

4. examples and analyses of weak, strong and exceptional responses

5. tips to strengthen the behavioural example

 ## INTERVIEW TIP

You are given examples of weak, strong and exceptional answers because many organizations will rate your answers (usually on a scale of 1-5) rather than just noting whether your response is good or bad. It would be easier to score exceptional if you knew how that differed from the weak and strong answers.

▶ **Leadership**

1. Recognizes opportunities and has vision to achieve them. Gains others' support for ideas and solutions and energizes them to work towards a common goal. Maximizes individual strengths and potential. Makes tough decisions.

2. Skill Level	Description
WEAK	▸ Has no vision; does not set directions ▸ Follows directions or prescribed instructions ▸ Participates as a member rather than leads ▸ Leads through fear ▸ Wants everyone to do things "one way"
STRONG	▸ Identifies opportunities ▸ Sets a direction for change ▸ Motivates others to take action
EXCEPTIONAL	▸ Sets a stretch vision ▸ Consistently selected by others to lead ▸ Inspires exceptional performance in others ▸ Anticipates and addresses potential obstacles ▸ Achieves exceptional results

3. **Various ways of asking the question:**

Tell me about a time when you...
  ▸ demonstrated strong leadership skills
  ▸ motivated others to achieve something significant
  ▸ led a group and got team support
  ▸ inspired others to overcome an obstacle

"Tell me about a time when you demonstrated strong leadership skills?"

4. Weak Answer:

I demonstrated strong leadership skills when I was a camp counsellor. I made sure I understood the process and policies for managing the children at the camp. I also made sure both the team and I knew the company mission and vision so that we all strived to achieve the same goals. As a camp counsellor, I would also let the children know the consequences for misbehaving in advance. This helped to deter misbehaviour significantly at camp. In addition, as a camp counsellor, I would occasionally think of new games for the children. The families were extremely happy with my leadership skills and the children would continue to participate in camp every summer.

Analysis

This answer is weak because the individual takes an established direction as a basis for a goal and does not try to achieve stretching results. It also appears that the individual follows procedures too closely and focuses on monitoring the children's behaviours rather than inspiring them. She also failed to discuss how the team is being motivated.

Strong Answer:

B As a camp counsellor, I noticed many children continued to misbehave despite numerous warnings of the consequences of misbehaving. This was a major problem because as camp counsellors we spent the majority of own time dealing with behavioural problems rather than creating a fun learning environment.

A I discussed my concerns with my team. They agreed that there was a problem; however they were very tired and de-motivated to make changes. I did not feel this was acceptable because I felt we had a higher responsibility to the children. I approached each camp counsellor individually and said, *"We are role models for these children, if we focus on the negatives, we will always be working against the children and not with the children. Let's start acting like their leaders and not the police. In the end our change in our approach will make our jobs easier and more enjoyable"*.

Within a few days, I was able to convince all five of the camp counsellors that we needed to brainstorm ways inspire the children to listen to us, have fun, learn and get along with each other. I initiated a group meeting to brainstorm ideas. As a group, we came up with many fun team-building activities that inspired the children to share and effectively play with each other. We also came up with rewards for each of these activities, gave children tools to help them resolve conflict on their own and devised a consistent process for dealing with individual misbehaviour. In addition, I asked my manager to provide positive feedback and incentives to the camp counsellors to keep them motivated. At the end of the summer, I also spear headed a reward ceremony to recognize the achievements of the children and counsellors.

R Many of the children stopped misbehaving. Instead they became more eager to participate in the many new team-building activities. The camp counsellors learned how to become leaders and enjoyed their jobs much more. My manager and the children's parents were ecstatic about the results.

Analysis

The answer is strong because the individual had a vision and aligned others to achieve it. She also recognized others' concerns and addressed them. This created an open and participatory environment. The individual also motivated her team achieve an extraordinary goal.

Exceptional Answer

B During my summer before the final year of University, I discovered the option of having a career in management consulting. However, I was shocked to find out that this opportunity was not widely-publicized and that there were no campus association or any resources available for students to learn about consulting. I also found out that many of the top management consulting firms did not actively recruit on this campus because the applicants were not considered to be very strong.

A I decided to start a Consulting Association. I talked to five other classmates who I knew were ambitious and discussed starting this student group with me. I convinced all of these students to join me by educating them about the benefits of a career in consulting and the challenges in obtaining a consulting job. I also appealed to their thirst to launch a start-up, noting that this experience would strengthen their résumé.

The campus recruiting season was at the beginning of the school year, I knew we had to act fast to get the organization started. I leveraged my experience as a past student leader to launch the association. First, I quickly put a list of tasks required to implement the new association; for example we had to get registered, get companies to come to campus, create students awareness all before September. I then encouraged my team mates to select activities they wanted to lead. Since each activity also had many components, I suggested we recruit additional committee members to help out. I held weekly Executive meetings to provide constant motivation to my team, to create an atmosphere of open communication and shared problem-solving and to ensure we anticipated potential obstacles. To make sure the team maintained high levels of motivation, I always began the meeting with the accomplishments to date and publicly recognized the individuals responsible for the accomplishments. Our support of one another and high accountability led us to achieve a lot in very little time.

R I lead the group as the Founding President in a team of 5 Executives and 20 Committee members. We signed up over 200 general members and offered our members free access to consulting events and a library filled with consulting resources. We also received support from five of the top tier management consulting firms in the form of sponsorships and free seminars/presentations. Our members became more aware of career opportunities in management consulting and the consulting firms were actively recruiting on our campus.

Analysis

The example is exceptional because the individual had a stretching vision — to create a new organization to fill a void - and she succeeded. She was successful in motivating and enabling others to achieve the goal with her and she was a major driving force to getting things accomplished quickly. By mentioning she had been a leader elsewhere she signalled her consistency in being an enabler. She anticipated and addressed upcoming obstacles. The outcome was exceptional because a new association was created to provide value to the University, the Consulting Firms and most of all the students.

5. How to get from Strong to Stronger:

‣ Show that you were *chosen* to be the leader

‣ Describe how your vision was stretching

‣ Show how you can *energize* a group of people

▶ **Risk-Taking**

1. Pursues potential opportunities that may result in positive results but may lead to negative consequences. Evaluates risks by weighing pros and cons; takes action in the face of uncertainties.

2. Skill Level	Description
WEAK	▸ Sets easily attainable goals ▸ Delays action ▸ Acts without evaluating risks
STRONG	▸ Sets challenging goals ▸ Takes action towards goals ▸ Seeks information to minimize risks
EXCEPTIONAL	▸ Sets stretch goals ▸ Demonstrates sense of urgency ▸ Evaluates risks and makes calculated decisions ▸ Is courageous in championing initiatives despite adversity and uncertainty ▸ Applies learnings to new experiences

3. Various ways of asking the question:

Tell me about a time when you...
  ▸ took a risk to achieve something significant
  ▸ took initiative and implemented something new
  ▸ set a challenging goal and was able to achieve it

"Tell me about a time when you had to take a risk to achieve something significant?"

4. Weak Answer:

One summer I had a job where I had to sell beauty salon coupons on the street. I got paid on commission only. It was my responsibility to decide where I wanted to sell. I didn't know which location to choose. This was a risk because if I picked the wrong location I would not get paid. I wanted to do a good job and get strong sales so I decided to do two things. First, I scheduled my sales days at the end of the summer, so I had time to do a geographic analysis to see where I could find more women who I thought would be more likely to make the purchases. I then asked some of my colleagues to see which area they thought would be better since they had more experience. Most people agreed on a few locations that were more likely to have people who would be interested in purchasing the beauty salon coupons. I took the location that matched most closely with my geographic analysis and it worked because I had strong sales compared to my colleagues.

Analysis

A good risk-taker evaluates the situation based on the information at hand and has a bias towards action. She would take the opportunity to learn and improve. Instead, this answer is weak because the individual delayed action until the last possible moment. Furthermore, the goal was not stretching nor was it specific.

Strong Answer:

B I had a summer job where I had to sell beauty salon coupons. My salary was based on 100% commission and I had to decide where and how I was going to sell these coupons. The risk was that if I did not sell, I would not get paid. Also, there was no place that was known to provide the best sales results. To minimize some of the risk of uncertainty, my colleagues wanted to go to together to do the sales and then split the money at the end of each day.

A I did not think selling the coupons together was a good idea. If the location was not good, switching locations would likely be slow and require group consensus. Furthermore, I wanted to sell more coupons than anyone else, not the same amount. However, I knew that if I went alone I would not be considered part of the team. In the end, I decided to take a risk and go by myself to one of the places where I thought I could potentially hit the high numbers. I 'set up shop' during hours when and at a location where there were a lot of people. I would approach both women and men to buy the coupons. I made sure I recorded my sales records each day for each locationbecause if a location or time was good, I would go back there. This really helped me make the sales.

R By the end of the summer, I had sold more than 15 coupons each day which was 50% more than what my colleagues sold.

Analysis

The answer is strong because the individual set a specific goal that was challenging yet attainable of exceeding peer results. She took action quickly and created information by tracking data to minimize risk. Although this was a strong example, the goals were not stretching and there was little demonstration of urgency.

Exceptional Answer:

B I had a summer job where I had to sell beauty salon coupons. My salary was based on 100% commission and I had to decide where and how I was going to sell these coupons. The risk was that if I did not sell, I would not get paid. I had only one month to sell the coupons and make enough money to go on a trip to Europe with my friends. If I did not sell enough, I would not get to go to Europe. Also, there was no place that was known to provide the best sales results.

A I felt that selling enough coupons to finance my trip in one month required a strategy. I decided to use the first couple days to quickly analyze historical sales' results and matched them with their corresponding locations. I then used the next few days to test out the locations identified as previously producing exceptional sales. I would use this experience to test my sales technique and gage demand for my product. If I didn't do well, I would have The time to think about why and adjust my sales pitch or change locations. This strategy was risky because by using the first week to analyze and test, I probably wasn't going to sell a lot. Because of that, a couple of the managers didn't like this initiative. However, I would likely learn a lot and hopefully sell more over the next three weeks to more than make up for my first week. I convinced my immediate manager of this so I was able to proceed with my plan.

As it turned out, my first couple of days were not so good. I noticed that when I did get sales, it was because of the type of people I was approaching. Younger women in their teens and twenties and surprisingly men over 30 tended to purchase the beauty salon coupons. In the remaining 3 weeks, I targeted these specific people.

R The plan worked! I made more than enough money to go to Europe. I became the top summer sales person in the company despite the fact that I only took one month to sell what my other new colleagues took the entire summer. In the end, I was asked to come back the following summer.

Analysis

This answer was exceptional because the individual took immediate action. In the face of adversity from some managers, she was courageous in championing an initiative. She took a calculated risk and set a stretching goal. By using the information she gathered and reapplying it to the situation, she quickly came up with a solid strategy to achieve exceptional results.

5. How to get from Strong to Stronger:

▸ Indicate the consequences of failing

▸ Demonstrate that you can learn from previous experiences and reapply information quickly

▸ Define your goal and ensure that it is set higher than what is normally achievable

▶ # Teamwork

1. Works cooperatively with diverse people to achieve common goals. Builds mutual respect and trust by listening and encouraging different points of views. Leverages individual members' strengths.

2. Skill Level	Description
WEAK	▸ Works competitively rather than co-operatively ▸ Prefers to work alone ▸ Does not seek out different perspectives ▸ Avoids conflict
STRONG	▸ Collaborates with others towards a common objective ▸ Values and elicits others' expertise and perspectives ▸ Respects, understands and trusts others ▸ Works to resolve conflict if present
EXCEPTIONAL	▸ Enables groups to work together rather than working in silos to achieve exceptional results ▸ Has strong influence on team outcomes without being perceived as dominant ▸ Brings out others strengths and leverages each person's area of expertise ▸ Creates an atmosphere of trust, mutual respect and open sharing ▸ Publicly recognizes others for their strong performance

3. **Various ways of asking the question:**

Tell me about a time when you...
   ▸ experienced a team conflict, what did you do
   ▸ were part of a team
   ▸ had to work with others that had different points of view from your own

"Tell me about a time when you were part of a team?"

4. Weak Answer:

In our sales team, the two senior members were always bickering at each other. They had a tendency to disagree with one another because they allowed their personal dislikes and agendas to get in the way. This affected morale and made it difficult for the team to finish a project on time. My role as the next senior person was to help the team work co-operatively despite this conflict. I did not want to make the situation worse so I never confronted the two people. Instead, to minimize the conflict, I would focus the team on the result we were supposed to be working towards and move conversation forward. This worked and we finished the project on time.

Analysis

Instead of helping the team become more collaborative the individual avoided conflict! She didn't seek to understand the different perspectives and never help the individuals resolve their differences. By not facing the situation, the individual didn't help improve team dynamics.

Strong Answer:

B Last year I joined a University Case Competition. It was a six-member team and we all came from different disciplines of study (finance, marketing, accounting and engineering). Our goal was to win the competition.

A Since I was the only one with previous case competition experience, I had a good idea of what worked and what did not work and so I lead the team. I recommended we each read the case individually, engage in a preliminary discussion about the issues and then split up the six case questions by each individuals' area of expertise. At the end, we would regroup to see how everything flowed together. A group member disagreed. He felt that it was important not to divide the work up but to complete each requirement of the case competition together. Before I stated to him reasons why I felt his recommendation would likely not work, I sought to understand his reasoning. I found out that he felt that this would be a faster way to work because it would eliminate the last step of seeing if everything flowed together. He felt that if we worked on all the sections together we would generate better ideas. He also shared with me that he felt he was not a "true expert" to take on one question alone. From my experience, the process of working on all the parts in a large group would likely take longer and lead to greater frustrations. However, I recognized that he made a good point that more ideas are generated in groups rather than alone. More importantly, I realized that his objection stemmed from not feeling confident in his own abilities. Instead of imposing my idea of what would work better, I proposed that we worked in pairs and each pair would be responsible for two questions. The group agreed.

R By pairing individuals up to do the work, the work was actually completed faster and at a better quality. The individual who had disagreed with me felt that his input was taken into consideration. In the end, we produced a very strong presentation and won the competition.

Analysis

The example is strong because even though the individual's experience told her that her process was probably the best method of approaching the task at hand, she did not exert her knowledge but listened to anther team members' point of view to come up with a solution that worked for everyone.

Exceptional Answer:

B Being in the sales department, I am always pitching ideas to retail buyers and and their team of experts (her managers, merchandising executives and shelving specialists) who came from different perspectives and had individual objectives. However, in order to make the sale, everyone must agree on a common plan. One example was when the marketing department of a category I sold wanted to have in-store shelf education to create a stronger feel of equity (almost like a "store within a store" type concept). The buyer wanted to grow the category, her manager wanted make sure it didn't hurt sales in other categories, the shelving expert had to make sure all the product suggestions fit properly and presented well on the shelf, the merchandising executive wanted to make sure it was easily executable, my consumer market researcher wanted permission to do pre and post in-store analysis but this couldn't interfere with the customers' shopping atmosphere. My marketing manager had to balance this priority and his other priorities that were on bigger accounts, and I wanted to sell more product.

A To create alignment in spite of the differences in perspectives and objectives, I spent a lot of time trying to understand the buyer and his team's points of view, what their goals were, why they could or couldn't do certain things, etc. I would bring these differences in perspectives and objectives to the surface and provide initial recommendations to meet everyone's needs. Of course, once I presented the initial plan, I solicited their feedback and together we fine tuned the plan. When the buyer had concerns or was unclear about the project, I invited my colleagues who were category managers and consumer research specialists to present product and con sumer behaviour research. I have a lot of faith in their abilities because they are experts and usually succeed in influencing the buyers' mind. When they saw that I also had an interest in ensuring their success, they were all more open to working together. I also publicly acknowledge any good ideas so that individuals would feel validated.

R In the end, fostering an atmosphere of trust and open communication with these various people brought best in class and first to market product executions. We all achieved our individual objectives while contributing to the collective goal. I grew the fastest that year compared to my colleagues on other accounts.

Analysis

This example is exceptional because the individual worked with a team of diverse backgrounds and goals and yet she was able to get everyone to work productively together to bring about uncommon results. She pro-actively sought people with expertise at the right time and she inspired trust through mutual respect. This example also demonstrated that she has exceptional skills at understanding others.

5. How to get from Strong to Stronger:

▸ Build common objectives by *gaining others trust*

▸ Form *productive relationships* that move toward a common goal

▸ Create *team results* that are *uncommonly strong*

▶ # Time Management

1. Prioritizes multiple responsibilities and deadlines effectively. Eliminates wasted efforts by knowing when and how to seek others' expertise. Breaks larger assignments into manageable chunks. Re-evaluates priorities on a regular basis. Spends time working on the most significant or time-sensitive tasks first. Finds improved ways of doing things to increase efficiency.

2. Skill Level	Description
WEAK	▸ Has no systematic way of managing time ▸ Avoids dealing with multiple responsibilities ▸ Handles tasks one at a time ▸ Comfortable with current processes even if inefficient ▸ Avoids dealing with complexity
STRONG	▸ Prioritizes and breaks assignments into manageable chunks ▸ Co-ordinates schedules with others to meet deadlines ▸ Delegates tasks appropriately ▸ Achieves balance between personal, academic and work objectives ▸ Consistently meets deadlines ▸ Finds improved ways of getting results
EXCEPTIONAL	▸ Is pro-active in anticipating needs and demands that may interrupt schedule ▸ Deals with time constraints creatively ▸ Adopts time saving measures without impacting quality ▸ Has exceptional ability to take on new initiatives and get them done ▸ Applies the 80-20 principle ▸ Not only meets deadlines but achieves high level of performance results ▸ Encourages others to develop their skills to improve overall efficiency

3. **Various ways of asking the question:**

    Tell me about a time when you...
    ▸ effectively balanced many competing activities
    ▸ had to pick out the most important tasks and ensure those
      were done properly
    ▸ manage a complex project and did so successfully

    ### *"Tell me about a time when you effectively balanced many competing activities?"*

4. **Weak Answer:**

Well, right now I have to do this. I have to balance school, a part-time job, being an executive on a student group, make time for friends and family and have time to myself. They are all important so I can't let anything drop. School basically comes first and I prioritize based on exams and project due dates. Then I schedule my work-time around it, and go to executive meetings. I tell my friends and family when I don't have time and they have to understand that at this time, other things need attention first. I'm getting good grades, doing well at work and have been able to contribute to the student group as well as still find time for my personal life - so I've been balancing all these different tasks pretty well.

Analysis

> The answer is weak because the example is common and the solution is not unique - many students face the same problems. The individual also did not look at how they could work more efficiently to reduce the amount of time spent on studying or helping the student group have more productive meetings. The individual does not demonstrate strong time management skills.

Strong Answer:

B As a student I always have to balance competing priorities. But this is a good thing because I have more energy when I have lots on my plate. Currently, I balance school, a part-time job, being an executive on a student group, volunteer as a big sister, as well as have time for my personal life like family and friends. They are all important so I can't let anything drop.

A To balance all these priorities, I make sure I'm not wasting time and a set a very disciplined schedule. For school, I avoid procrastinating by doing my readings every night or assignments everyday before final deadlines. I also initiated a study group and in this group we divide up practice questions and exchange our answers. This way, we do not have to work on all of the assigned questions but still have all the answers.

I also make sure that my student group meetings occur immediately after everyone's classes so that we don't have to spend time commuting to school on another day just to meet. Sometimes, these meetings would occur during lunch or dinner since we all have to eat anyway. It is also important for me that in team work that we all get equal parts to work on and hence we delegate responsibilities appropriately.

I volunteer on weekends in the early morning so that I could free time in the afternoon for other activities or work at my part-time job.

R I'm getting good grades. I always meet deadlines. I am doing well at work and have been able to contribute to the student group as well as still find time for my personal life — so I've been balancing all these different tasks pretty well.

Analysis

This response is beyond the typical response, "I have lots to do, and I'm getting it done so I must be doing good!" The individual also demonstrated some techniques to manage her time in personal, academic and extracurricular settings. However, examples of more systematic ways to reduce inefficiencies would strengthen this response.

Exceptional Answer:

B I recognize that many students struggle with finding enough time to do everything, however, I believe that my tasks go beyond what a typical student has to deal with. Not only am I a full-time student, but I am also launching a new student group for the first time and working part-time in a business I started with a friend. I also participate on the Case Competition Team which requires me to attend case review practices on a regular basis. Beyond all this, I also have friends and family, which also need my attention and time; it is through their support that I draw the energy to do so much.

A With all that being said, aside from making sure I do not procrastinate with school, I balance these priorities by always seeking to improve efficiencies. For example, when launching the new student group, I sought out advice on best practices from people who had previously worked on other student groups. I also encouraged my team members to do the same. This helped everyone save time because we did not have to "reinvent the wheel".

With regards to the partnership with my friend, I noticed that at the beginning of our working relationship we spent a lot of time brainstorming and giving feedback to each other. In the end, it would take us a long time to agree on something and get things done. I suggested we meet less frequently, but that each time we do meet, we had to have more things done. We were able to move along with our business plan more quickly after this.

For the case competition team, I noticed that none of us had other commitments right after class. Instead of finding another time like the weekend to meet and having to travel to and from campus again, I suggested we meet after the class and save the commute time.

For my social life, I would initiate group get-togethers as oppose to one-on-one activities. The time spent with each individual person is less, but I get to catch up with more people at once and that's good too.

R My results to date have been very good. I founded a student group that has put on more events than any other group in the same time period. The business my friend and I are starting is set to launch in a few weeks. I'm getting strong grades and my case competition team has already won one tournament. Above all, I'm staying in touch with all my friends and having a great time doing everything.

Analysis

The answer is exceptional because the individual demonstrate an extraordinary ability to handle many tasks at once and perform them well. She is involved in a variety of things, each one beyond surface participation. She actively seek to learn how to work more efficiently and is very proactive in managing new demands. Not only did she save herself time, but she also helped others save time and encourage others to do the same.

5. How to get from Strong to Stronger:

▸ Identify ways to make *complex tasks easier to handle*

▸ Describe a few *significant tasks* rather than list many trivial tasks

▸ Find ways to *improve other's capacities* and therefore your own

▶ **Analytical Thinking**

1. Ability to think critically and breaks situation into smaller pieces to organize thoughts/process in a step-by-step approach. Analyzes data, creates alternatives and uses a logical approach to problem solving. Clearly identifies patterns in complex and unorganized data. Finds relationships between seemingly unrelated issues.

2. Skill Level	Description
WEAK	▸ Has difficulties sorting through complex data and identifying key issues ▸ Has experience with relatively simple problems or unable to solve complex problems ▸ Lacks systematic approach in problem solving; uses a trial and error approach ▸ Selects from a limited number of pre-established responses
STRONG	▸ Sorts through complex data and identifies relevant points ▸ Identifies sources and symptoms of problems ▸ Quickly grasps critical issues in a problem and develops solutions ▸ Analyzes data to create alternatives ▸ Usually questions assumptions ▸ Interprets data to identify possibly emerging problems
EXCEPTIONAL	▸ Does not accept information at face value but probes to understand the data ▸ Evaluates and interprets complex, controversial or obscure information, identify gaps and derives relevant meaning ▸ Proposes alternative approaches to unfamiliar situations or concepts ▸ Interprets the impact of potential solutions on external elements ▸ Creates precedent-setting solutions

3. **Various ways of asking the question:**

Tell me about a time when you…
▸ showcased your analytical skills
▸ solved a complex problem using logic and reasoning
▸ analyzed complex data, sorted through alternatives and quickly came up with a solution
▸ faced a difficult problem and solved it

"Tell me about a time when you showcased your analytical skills?"

4. **Weak Answer:**

For a symbolic logic philosophy course, I had to always solve complex problems. I solved these problems by using deduction and inference techniques. The problems got more complex as the year progressed, but I got one of the top marks in the class.

Analysis

This is a weak example because the individual only used prescribed methods for problem-solving.

Strong Answer:

B As part of a course, I had to work in a four person team to analyze a business case study. The case had a number of complex issues the team had to resolve. We needed to understand why the company was losing market share, had cash flow shortage, and increased consumer complaints.

A To help the group work through this problem, I suggested that for each problem area, we would identify:
▸ key issues
▸ assumptions
▸ contributing factors to the problems
▸ areas to improve and potential solutions.

My main contribution to the group was sorting through many complex financial statements. In my analysis, I realized the cash flow problem resulted from the company's recent decision to expand their R&D department. They had spent a lot of money purchasing new equipment.

We then discussed everyone's thoughts and assumptions and came up with a solution to reverse the strategy.

R We completed the analysis in one week. We presented our project in the form of a skit where each member would take on the role of a Manager representing the four affected functional areas. Our audience would be the Board Members and the Professor would be the Chairman and CEO of the company. We demonstrated a strong understanding of our case and got an A on the assignment.

Analysis

This was a strong answer because the individual sorted through a massive array of complex information by questioning assumptions to uncover key problem areas. She broke the case into smaller organized pieces, analyzed alternatives which enabled the team to understand the issues and develop a solution. This response could have been strengthened if the individual also presented recommendations to solve the issues.

Exceptional Answer:

B As part of a course, I had to work in a four person team to analyze a business case study. The case had a number of complex issues the team had to resolve. We needed to understand why the company was losing market share, had cash flow shortage, and increased consumer complaints.

A To help the group work through this problem, I suggested that for each problem area, we would identify:
  ‣ key issues
  ‣ assumptions
  ‣ contributing factors to the problems
  ‣ areas to improve and potential solutions.

My main contribution was the financial statements analysis. I correlated trends in revenues and profits versus various changes in expenses. By doing that, I noticed a change in the company focus from shifting labour expenses in their marketing department to their R&D department two years prior. Furthermore, there was increase in R&D equipment. This one change in focus resulted in all the problem areas identified earlier. The shortage of cash flow resulted from the R&D capital investments which did not bring immediate returns on investment. Furthermore, since that change, the company's share started declining and consumer complaints skyrocketed.

We then discussed everyone's thoughts and assumptions and came up with a solution to reverse the strategy.

R We were the only team to propose reversing a historical decision and increase people costs to increase profits. All the other teams suggested separate solutions for each department. As a result, our team was the only one that cracked the case and received an A!

Analysis

This answer was exceptional because it took the strong answer one step further by finding the underlying cause behind all the issues. The individual did not accept the information at face value and probed further.

5. How to get from Strong to Stronger:

▸ Show that the problem or issue was complex or multi-dimensional

▸ Show that you considered many alternatives, evaluated the potential impact and selected the best solution

▸ Use an example where you analyzed data and not just facts

▶ **Creative Thinking**

1. Curious, imaginative and thinks "outside the box". Consistently pursues innovative and new learning. Explores new or recombines knowledge to generate novel and valuable solutions. Uses intuition and looks beyond status quo to create new insights.

2. Skill Level	Description
WEAK	▸ Tends to be narrow in thinking or resistance to change ▸ Uncomfortable with novel ideas or approaches ▸ Follows precedent rather than generates new solutions ▸ Fear of mistakes prevents action
STRONG	▸ Has a broad view and open to change ▸ Asks "Why?" ▸ Tries new approaches to get better results ▸ Imports solutions from outside environment
EXCEPTIONAL	▸ Takes action to change perspectives or break from status quo ▸ Asks "What if?" ▸ Combines knowledge in new ways to solve old problems ▸ Generates new ideas that are not constrained by traditional views ▸ Imports and modifies solutions from outside environment ▸ Creates new theory

3. **Various ways of asking the question:**

Tell me about a time when you…
- ‣ overcame something you thought was impossible and how you did it
- ‣ came up with a new idea and got it executed
- ‣ solved a problem in a unique way

"Tell me about a time that you came up with a new idea and got it executed?"

4. Weak Answer:

I was in charge of organizing an end of summer party at work. My supervisor put me in charge of all the logistics, budgets and ultimately all the decisions. I wanted to come up with a theme for the party so I asked my colleagues for input. No one was able to give me any compelling ideas but in the end, I came up with the theme of having a "Summer Blockbuster Costume Party". This party originally required everyone to dress up as a character from the summer blockbuster hits. Some people loved the idea and others were not so keen. To avoid rocking the boat, I made wearing a costume optional. Although not everyone dressed up in costumes, everyone loved the party. My manager commended me on creating a fun and unique night!

Analysis

The individual had a creative idea of a summer blockbuster custom party but she failed to fully realize it. Her fear of "rocking the boat" prevented her from taking action to generate excitement from her colleagues. There was some evidence of creativity but it wasn't very stretching.

Strong Answer:

B As part of my summer internship at a real estate company, I had to organize their annual end of summer party. I was in charge of all the logistics, budgets and all the decisions. I learned that in previous years, the party was usually dinner at a hotel or restaurant, games and raffles and ended with music and small dance. Usually about half the people came. I decided I wanted to create something unique and exciting so that more people would come out.

A I asked people who didn't come out previous years why they didn't. Some people said they would rather spend time with their family, others said they just weren't interested because its just dinner at a fancy restaurant and nothing too special. Understanding everyone's concerns, I expanded the purpose of the event from simply a bonding and fun opportunity to a celebratory event. We would celebrate the results of the year as well individual accomplishments. Five awards were to be given out and I invited the local paper to cover the event. They would print pictures of the evening and winners in their paper. The event was to be held on a boat instead of an indoor restaurant so people could enjoy the summer in a unique setting. To further encourage attendance, I invited everyone to bring a guest. That would allow those who wanted to spend time with their family to bring a part of their family to dinner. Because increasing guests meant increasing costs, I had to cut elsewhere. Instead of hiring a band, I brought a guest who was an amateur DJ who would simply manage the music for the evening.

R In the end the event was really successful - we had about 80% attendance, but it was much bigger than previous years because of the extra guests. Everyone was really excited about the boat and the talk about the evening continued the following week because the newspaper coverage the came out. A plaque for each award was created at work so that each year's winners would be engraved on the wall. As those plaques get updated, it also motivated people to want to achieve better results too!

Analysis

This was a very strong answer because the individual was open to change from the beginning and didn't want to just replicate. She also asked a lot of "why" questions to understand how to improve the situation. Finally, she tried a new approach and got better results.

Exceptional Answer:

B While I was on an exchange in Africa, I volunteered my time at an orphanage. This orphanage was severely under-funded. I made it my mission to help the orphanage receive adequate funding to carry out its activities.

A At first I thought of traditional ways to raise money for a good cause. Such as have bake sales, lobby the government and solicit private donors. However, I realized that this form of fundraising was not sustainable. Someone else would have to continue doing what I would have done, and this was not possible because no one at the orphanage had the skills to lobby the government or get private funding. There was also no money to hire a dedicated fundraiser. This was a huge and common problem among non-profits in Africa. Then I realized that instead of trying to raise as much money as I could, I needed to create a self-sustaining system to generate regular cash flow. My idea involved partnering with local schools and other non-profit agencies in the community. We would create a program where local children would learn to be entrepreneurs. The students would run a store (of their choice), create products to sell etc. as part of their learning and 50% of the proceeds will go to fund the orphanage. It would be like Junior Achievement! This took a lot of hard work. I had to generate buy-in and recruit and train young entrepreneurs. I also had to lobby the govern ment to get continual funding for the entrepreneurship program.

R In the end, the fundraising initiative was very successful. The young entrepre neurs gained newfound confidence and business skills. The orphanage received $5,000 in new money. This program now happens once a year with new students. Students are gaining business skills, the orphanage is gener- ating regular cash flow and the local community is strengthening because it's laid the seed for a more highly skilled workforce.

Analysis

This was an exceptional answer because instead of just finding ways to meet the current needs of the orphanage, the individual thought of ways to help the orphanage self-sustain. This idea goes beyond what is expected and helps the orphanage break away from the status quo. The individual also borrowed from a well-established idea in North America (Junior Achievement) and took it one step further by channelling the proceeds to non-profits. In the end, the individual did more than just raise money for the orphanage, but she also created a new theory of self-sustainability for non-profits. Everyone in the system benefits and the local economy was enriched in this process.

5. How to get from a Strong to Stronger

▸ Show that you *questioned* an existing practice or approach

▸ Show that you *applied knowledge from another area to solve your current challenge*

▸ Show that the outcome *transformed* others' way of thinking or action

▶ **Ethics**

1. Consistently and without exception exhibits high standards of fairness and integrity when dealing with others. Does not jeopardize others' interests for personal benefits. Is trusted and respected by others. Does not compromise sound principles, values and standards under any circumstances.

2. Skill Level	Description
WEAK	▶ Aware of the importance of ethical behaviour and its impact on trust and influence ▶ Behaviours are inconsistent ▶ Sees potential conflicts of interests but just tries to minimize severity
STRONG	▶ Exemplifies high standards of honest and ethical behaviours ▶ Effectively manages conflicts of interest ▶ Avoids action or statements that compromise integrity
EXCEPTIONAL	▶ Sticks to principles even when unpopular to do so ▶ Takes responsibility for failures and mistakes without blaming others or circumstances ▶ Models and encourages ethical behaviours ▶ Earns and maintains the trust of others by acting consistently ▶ Proactive in safeguarding integrity and principles ▶ Prevents situations of conflicts of interests from coming up

3. **Various ways of asking the question:**

    Tell me about a time when you...
    ‣ were asked to do something you didn't think
      was right and how you handled it.
    ‣ found yourself in a position of a conflict of interest
      and how you handled it.
    ‣ did not compromise your own integrity even though
      it may have been tempting.

"Tell me about a time when you found yourself in a position of a conflict of interest and how you handled it?"

4. **Weak Answer:**

I was the President of the Consulting Association, and we ran a case competition where we asked company representatives to participate as judges. Any student who was interested could enter. If there were more submissions than space provided, we would take entries on a first-come-first serve basis. The competition provided not only a learning experience, but also exposure to recruiters. The winners of the case competition would get noticed by the consulting firm and would be able to highlight the achievement on their résumés. Some of the executives wanted to enter into the competition (I also did). However, this was a conflict of interest because all the Executives including myself had previous exposure to the judges, a good understanding of how the event would be structured and what type of case we were looking to find. Furthermore, if we had to turn some students away because of space constraints, we might be looked at negatively by other students who assumed we gave ourselves preferential treatment. However, I didn't know which case was actually going to be chosen. I thought about it and decided that other students could also have gone to information seminars and had exposure to the company representatives. Other students may also have had exposure to case competitions as well. Just because I was part of the executive team should not prevent me or any of the other executives from a learning experience as well. So we entered the competition, but we published the list of participants so that everyone knew that we were competing as well and it wasn't hidden. I had another executive on the team who did not want to participate choose the case study, and I didn't look at it until the competition began. So I felt that everyone was on equal footing.

Analysis

The answer is weak because the individual compromised the interest of other students for her own benefit. Knowing that the case competition was something that the student group was going to organize, she could have put measures in place to prevent as much of the conflict of interest as possible. The Executives should have decided from the beginning whether they would participate, and if they did want to, they could have agreed not to have exposure to the organization for this specific activity. Deciding after the fact was not fair to others.

Strong Answer:

<u>B</u> I had a part-time job conducting telephone surveys. New hires started off at $7/hour and you could eventually work yourself up to $10/hour depending on your results and your seniority. Many of the other people there had been there for a couple years. For each 4 hour shift we had to hit a quota of at least 5 full interviews. On average, it took about 10 minutes to complete a full interview, however the target was only 5 interviews per shift because you would get a lot of people who weren't at home, didn't want to do the survey, didn't qualify to participate in the survey or who terminated the survey partway. Many times, I would see the other workers talk on the phone with friends, chat with other co-workers, and then even fake some of the research surveys.

<u>A</u> I would usually just go through my 4-hour shift and work non-stop, not even for the 15-minute break that I was allowed to take because I didn't feel I needed it in only 4 hours. Instead, I exceed quotas and was the top surveyor of each of the shifts I worked. Eventually, one of my colleagues came up to me and bluntly asked me why I was making life so difficult for everyone. He said that because of the number of surveys I completed, I made everyone else look bad and it was even worse that I was new. He said that I made things even worse by not even taking my break. I listened to him and asked him whether he knew new hires started at only $7/hour. He said he did. He had been working there for sometime so because of the pay system, I gathered that he and most everyone else made more than me. I explained that I needed money, and that's why I took a part-time job. I explained that I wanted to make the $10/hour that most other people here was making, but in order to do that, I needed to get strong results. I spent the time to understand where he was coming from and agreed to start taking my 15-minutes breaks. I then took the time to explain my situation to him so that he understood where I was coming from too.

R I didn't change my work ethics to match theirs because I didn't think what they were doing was right. I still had the best results, and I got the pay increases I wanted because of it.

Analysis

The answer is strong because the individual did not take the easy route to jeopardize the integrity of the organization's results. She confronted the problem and continued to do the right thing in the face of little support from her peers.

Exceptional Answer:

B This year I founded a Consulting Association for students. We decided early on that we wanted to create a Case Competition at the university. Knowing that some of the executives would want to participate, I saw the potential of a conflict of interest.

A To prevent this from happening, I asked each executive to tell me up front if they wanted to participate, and I made sure these individuals did not have any exposure or influence on the case competition. They were to be treated the same as any other student. They would not know what type of case was going to be used; they would not know who the judges were going to be, etc. When the sign up for the competition started, it was going to be on a first-come-first-serve basis until all the spots were filled. The list was also to be updated publicly so everyone knew which executives were going to participate. We would also print a disclaimer indicating the Executives had no influence on the competition. It was difficult because some of the executives pushed back. They thought that as executives of the association, they should be part of the planning process. I explained that other students may be upset if they thought any of the participants had any unfair advantage. The integrity of the competition would have been jeopardized, as well as the credibility of our group. The recruiters who would be judging the contest may also be unimpressed. I knew this last point was important to them because they wanted to impress the recruiters so they agreed.

R I think conflicts of interests come up all the time, but the important thing is to try and prevent it, minimize as much of it as possible and fully disclose the conflict to all potentially interested parties.

Analysis

The answer is exceptional because the individual not only did the right thing she helped others learn to do the right thing as well. She anticipated the conflict of interest and prevented it from occurring by proactively putting measures in place to minimize as well as fully disclose the conflict. She stuck to her decision not to involve the executives in the planning of the case competition even though they resisted.

5. How to get from Strong to Stronger:

▸ *Anticipate conflicts of interest* in advance and find ways to minimize it

▸ Demonstrate *using your principles* as your guide in decision making

▸ Demonstrate you *stuck to what you believed* in even though you had little to no support

▶ **Initiative**

1. Takes action without being prompted by others or with minimum direction, support or approval. Recognizes alternatives to potential problems before they become obvious.

2. Skill Level	Description
WEAK	▸ Carries out tasks that are expected ▸ May raise issues for improvements ▸ Understands the need to seek improvement but does not take action until request is made
STRONG	▸ Takes action to resolve problems without waiting to be asked ▸ Anticipates future needs or opportunities and proposes action plan to achieve desired results ▸ Is comfortable taking risks and challenging way things are done
EXCEPTIONAL	▸ Strives to achieve goals beyond what is required ▸ Anticipates and acts on changes, trends or emerging issues ▸ Challenges the way things are done and takes action towards improvements ▸ Proactively leads new projects; inspires and involves others to take on new initiatives ▸ Completes initiative even when it becomes difficult

3. **Various ways of asking the question:**

Tell me about a time when you…
   ▸ went above and beyond the call of duty in order to get a job done
   ▸ demonstrated initiative and caused a change to occur
   ▸ anticipated potential problems and developed preventive measures

> implemented a project or idea (not necessarily your own) that was successful primarily because of your efforts
> took on a project or role that was outside your job description

"Give me an example of a time you seized an opportunity and took action?"

4. Weak Answer:

As an account representative I had received a compliant from a client who was angry because we had delivered the wrong package to her home for the second time. In response I took the initiative to thoroughly investigate the situation. I looked up the client record to verify the order. The order was correct so I called up the delivery department to find out why the wrong package was sent. Apparently, I found out that there was a mix up in product codes. I flagged this to my manager's attention so that something like this would not occur again in the future. In the end, I was able to correct the mistake for the client by sending her the correct package. Also, to thank her for being patient with our organization, I sent her a few product samples and discount coupons.

Analysis

The response is weak because the example given was an expected part of the individual's job! The individual was just "putting out fires" and not anticipating them in advance. While the source of the problem was identified, ways of preventing it from reoccurring was not explored. Using the word "initiative" in your response is not enough.

Strong Answer:

B I was hired as a summer student to perform telemarketing calls to sell news paper subscriptions. This was my first job and I received very little training, so I saw the need for a more extensive training program. I expressed my enthusiasm to develop this to my manager. At first he disagreed because he wanted me to focus on selling. I eventually convinced him otherwise and we negotiated that if I exceeded my sales quotas by at least 10% overall for two months, I could work with him to develop a training program to improve my team members' sales.

A To exceed the sales goals, I not only worked extremely hard but I stayed late (without extra pay) to achieve my sales targets. In addition, I documented my techniques to help improve my own sales and planned to use this information as the foundation for my training and marketing plan. Specifically, I wrote down the objections received from clients, how I responded and whether my responses helped closed the deal. My hard work and more strategic approach paid off. I exceeded sales quota by 20% for the month and this allowed me to devote time to develop a training and marketing plan for my team. I put the training and marketing plan together in a week and presented this to my colleagues. My training involved how to prospect clients within 1 minute, how to deal with rejections, and how to close the deal.

R At the end of the summer, not only was I able to exceed my own personal work targets, I developed a training and marketing plan that enabled others to do the same. In fact, together in one summer my team sold 50% more subscriptions than usual after receiving my training and when they administered the incentives I arranged. My manager was so impressed that I was offered a full-time job as a Senior Telemarketer/ Trainer. However, at the time I was going back to school so I declined the offer. The company then offered me flexible part-time employment, which I could not refuse!

Analysis

This is a strong answer. The individual took control of her summer experience and sought work outside of her job description, accomplishing more than what was expected of a summer employee. In addition, her initiative in the training and development area caused others to benefit from her expertise. Although this answer is strong, it could be strengthened if the individual involved her colleagues in the process.

Exceptional Answer:

B I was hired as a summer telemarketer to sell newspaper subscriptions. This was my first job and I received very little training. While this position was to focus on sales, which alone would still have made a good summer experience, I wanted to do more than just sell. I knew I could contribute more and I wanted to develop other skill sets. So when I saw the need for a more extensive training program, I expressed my enthusiasm to develop this to my manager. At first he disagreed because he wanted me to focus on selling. I eventually convinced him otherwise and we negotiated that if I exceeded my sales quotas by at least 10% overall for two months, I could work with him to develop a training program to improve my team's sales.

A To exceed the sales goals, when I got better results I would think about why that was the case so I could replicate it. I noticed that usually I got better results when I stepped out of the traditional "telemarketer" role of asking for a "Mr./Mrs. Smith" and then speed reading through a script before he/she had a chance to hang up on me. Instead, I had to be more casual (actually using people's first names) and be upfront that I was a tele-marketer, but truly had a great offer and ask for permission to tell them about it. People found my approach refreshing and were more willing to listen. I documented my techniques so that I could later use this information as the foundation for my training and. Specifically, I would write down the objections received from clients, how I responded and whether my responses help closed the deal. I also noticed another colleague who was also very successful. I asked him how he was able to achieve the results he got, and used some of his techniques myself. My hard work and more strategic approach paid off. I exceeded sales quota by 20% for the month and this allowed me to devote time to develop a training and plan for my team. Because the previous help from my colleague was so beneficial, I asked several other colleagues for their tips. With their input, I was able to create a much more robust training and tips program than I could have by myself. I presented the training plan to my manager. My training involved how to break away from the traditional telemarketer image, prospect clients within 1 minute, how to deal with rejections, and how to close the deal.

R At the end of the summer, not only was I able to exceed my own personal work targets, I developed a training and that enabled others to do the same. In fact, together in one summer my team sold 50% more subscriptions than usual after receiving my training and when they administered the incentives I arranged. My manager was so impressed that I was offered a full-time job as a Senior Telemarketer/ Trainer. However, at the time I was going back to school so I declined the offer. The company then offered me flexible part-time employment, which I could not refuse!

Analysis

This was an exceptional answer. The individual recognized a need to change how things were traditionally done and took steps to facilitate that change. She proactively sought others expertise and went above and beyond her role description to create a tool which enabled others to better succeed.

5. How to get from Strong to Stronger:

▸ Show that you *anticipated* a problem and took action

▸ Show that you *involved others* in the process

▸ Show that you performed *outside of your role* to achieve a desired outcome

▶ # Communication

1. Presents information in a clear and concise manner. Effectively gets others to open up by actively listening, asking appropriate questions and responding appropriately. Is persuasive.

2. Skill Level	Description
WEAK	▶ Unable to influence others ▶ Muffled/hesitant/stammering speech ▶ Pays attention when others talk and takes notes when appropriate ▶ Does not ask questions to understand others point of view
STRONG	▶ Conveys information, ideas, thoughts and feelings in a clear and professional manner ▶ Influences others ▶ Seeks to ensure facts are clearly understood ▶ Listens actively, reads body language and subtle messages
EXCEPTIONAL	▶ Ability to persuade others and sell ideas ▶ Seeks to understand, then to be understood ▶ Understands others' underlying needs, interests, issues and motivators ▶ Catches and interprets conflicting messages or actions ▶ Adapts style, words and action depending on audience ▶ Identifies barriers to communication and takes action to facilitate mutual understanding ▶ Explains complex concepts, thoughts and ideas clearly and concisely to all levels ▶ Challenges others' ideas tactfully while managing disagreements constructively

3. Various ways of asking the question:

    Tell me about a time when you…
    ‣ had to resolve a disagreement with a colleague
    ‣ gave an important presentation to a group of people
    ‣ persuaded someone to change their mind or do something they did
      not want to do

    ### *"Give me an example of a time you persuaded someone to change their mind?"*

4. Weak Answer:

Working at the campus book store we had a self-scheduling system whereby all the employees took turns to sign up for desirable shifts. Each person had to work at least 3 days a week. I was 5th in line to sign up for shifts and desperately need to take Saturday off to go to my grandfather's 65th birthday. Unfortunately, being 5th in line, Saturday became a mandatory shift for me because too many other people already took other shifts. What I did was approach each person who was not working Saturday to see if they would be willing to change shifts with me and that I would owe them next time if I took a day off that they wanted to take. At first I could not find anyone to trade shifts with me. Finally with some persistence and sacrifice, I convinced one person by trading with them two of my desirable shifts instead of one desirable shift next time. The result was I was able to go to my grandfather's birthday.

Analysis

The outcome was achieved not by using communication skills to convince another person through reason or persuasion, rather by giving them a "better deal". There was no evidence that the individual actively inquired or listened about other people's needs or wants.

Strong Answer:

B Working at the campus book store we had a self-scheduling system where all the employees took turns to sign up for desirable shifts. Each person had to work at least 3 days a week. I was 5th in line to sign up for shifts and desperately need to take Saturday off to go to my grandfather's 65th birthday. Unfortunately, being 5th in line, Saturday became a mandatory shift for me because too many other people already took other shifts.

A I approached each person who was not working Saturday to see if we could exchange shifts. I asked what they were doing during the weekend to understand if that day off was important to them too. As it turns out, only one person who didn't originally want to work that Saturday was actually free. I then chatted more with her to see what her plans were for the rest of the summer and found out she wanted to go to a couple of weddings. Finally, I explained to her my situation, and asked if she would be willing to trade shifts with me. I also offered that I didn't have any other major plans for the rest of summer, and that I would willingly trade shifts with her if necessary so she could attend both weddings.

R Because she understood my situation, because I wasn't asking her to give up anything she also had planned, and because I understood what was important to her and could offer her help if needed, she agreed to make the switch with me and I was able to attend my grandfather's birthday!

Analysis

This was a strong answer. The individual first sought to understand the rest of her colleagues' situation. She then targeted her time at her most likely candidate. She spent time to further understand this specific colleague's needs and delivered a customized answer that incorporated the other person's needs. This demonstrated to the other colleague she was listening. Her communication skills enabled her to achieve a desirable outcome.

Exceptional Answer:

B I had a disagreement with a more senior Operations Manager about hiring an existing contracted employee from a temporary agency to fill a full-time position with greater responsibilities. This manager was experiencing enormous pressure to fill the position because of increased workload in his department. I had agreed to interview the individual and other external candidates with the manager. Our goal was to find the best person for the job. The contracted candidate did not interview well, however we both agreed that one of the other candidates interviewed had exceptional skills. The disagreement arose because the manager wanted to hire the contracted candidate over the exceptional candidate.

A I asked the manager why he preferred the contracted employee and he said he thought she was the best option because she already knew the job. His concern was that the exceptional candidate would require extensive training and that he did not have the time or resources for this. In recognizing this, I asked him to tell me his short and longer term needs. I found out that in the long run, he needed someone who could not only be able to do the job but who could create efficiencies in the department or model behaviours he desired. However, his immediate need was to have someone who could start the job with minimal training. Through our conversation, I finally under stood where he was coming from. Having this insight, I told him that if he wanted the longer term outcome, he had to invest now to see returns sooner. I also offered him an option to keep the contracted candidate for a few months if he agreed to hire the exceptional candidate.

R In the end, he realized that it made more sense to invest in the long term. He agreed to hire the exceptional candidate and I agreed to extend the contracted candidates' term until the new hire was operating at full capacity. After a few months, the manager realized that he made the right decision because his department started operating more efficiently.

Analysis

This was an exceptional answer because the individual challenged someone who was at a higher level. By openly discussing the conflict, she was able to better understand the managers' needs and was able to identify the under-lying reason behind the conflict. With the understanding of the managers' concerns, she offered him a solution that best met his needs. This conflict was managed constructively and the outcome was positive for both the individual and the manager.

5. How to get from Strong to Stronger:

▸ Show that you *considerd in the other person's perspective*

▸ Show that you *managed disagreements effectively*

▸ Show that the *issue* under discussion was *important*

▶ **Results-Oriented**

1. Sets ambitious goals and demonstrates resiliency in achieving them. Tracks progress in meeting objectives, set priorities and overcomes barriers to completing tasks. Has high level of commitment to start and complete projects, even in the face of adversity. Focuses on end result and not on individual styles of achieving results. Self disciplined, success oriented and has tenacity.

2. Skill Level	Description
WEAK	▸ Produces only what is required ▸ Explores how to deliver additional work outcomes when requested ▸ Requires direction and supervision ▸ Won't work with difficult personalities ▸ Unwilling to make sacrifices to get results
STRONG	▸ Can work with difficult personalities ▸ Accomplishes priorities through careful planning and execution ▸ Makes some sacrifices in time/plans/energy for the sake of a work objective ▸ Anticipates, recognizes and seize opportunities
EXCEPTIONAL	▸ Makes personal sacrifices in order to reach goal ▸ Has strong sense of urgency ▸ Perseveres over extended period of time to overcome significant obstacles ▸ Stretches self and others to pursue difficult but possible goals ▸ Consistently attempts to improve vs. past results ▸ Focus on solution rather than process — see barriers as something to overcome as opposed to a reason to stop

3. **Various ways of asking the question:**

Tell me about a time when you...
▸ set an important goal and succeeded in reaching it
▸ achieved a great deal in a short amount of time
▸ surmounted a major obstacle to achieving a goal

"Give me an example of a time you set an important goal and succeeded in reaching it?"

4. Weak Answer:

In my final year as an undergrad, I decided I wanted to get a Masters degree. I was worried that it would be difficult because I made this decision only one month before the applications were due so I did not truly understand what all the criteria were. At the very last minute, while managing my coursework and extracurricular activities, I had to study very hard to write the GRE, complete the application forms, obtain references and prepare for the admissions interviews. To increase my chances of getting accepted, I applied to many different schools. In the end, even though it was hectic, I managed everything and was accepted into a couple different school.

Analysis

The individual did what was needed and got what she wanted. The answer was a list of things she had to do to get into the Masters program. Nothing significant was done.

Strong Answer:

B In my final year as an undergrad, I decided I wanted to get a Masters degree. However, I was told directly by the Administrator that my marks were not competitive and that I should not apply since only 20 spots were available for the top students.

A I took this criticism seriously and instead of becoming upset at the Administrator, I asked her for ways in which my application could be made more competitive. She told me that I not only needed high marks but I needed to obtain relevant experience for the program. I studied very hard and was able to achieve stellar marks in my final semester. Unfortunately, I later found out these marks were not officially released in time for the program's application review committee. I immediately conveyed my concerns to the Administrator and convinced her to accept my unofficial final marks. We agreed that if my Professors agreed to send the unofficial marks to her within a week's time she would accept them. In addition, as part of the application process, I had to submit a résumé. My résumé out lined my work experiences and extracurricular activities however I felt this two page summary did not allow the applicant review committee to truly understand my motivations for applying to the program. Although not required, I included a 3 page statement of interest outlining why the selection committee should select me, how I came to choose the program, and how I hope to contribute to the program. In this statement of interest, I tied all my experiences work, paid and volunteer together to form a story of how my career goals emerged. In addition, I included a summary of all my research papers to demonstrate I was capable of doing research.

R Everything I did helped me to stand out from the crowd and in the end, I got accepted to two graduate programs and received entrance scholarships for both programs!

Analysis

This is a strong example because despite being told not to apply to the program by the program administrator, the individual relentlessly pursued this goal by taking action beyond what was expected. The goal was also difficult because there were limited spots and she was not initially perceived as being competitive. In addition, the individual got into the program because she was able to anticipate the needs of the selection committee.

Exceptional Answer:

B I was a new graduate from a Human Resources program with limited work experience and absolutely no recruitment experience. I was hired for a 3 month contract as a recruiter while the organization was finding a perm- anent replacement for the role. This role was plagued with challenges and the most immediate one was the need to fill five difficult to hire positions that were vacant for at least one month. The Operations Managers were frustrated and extremely dissatisfied.

A The first thing I did was establish my three immediate goals. I presented these goals to my own manager to ensure that I was on the right track. My first goal was to alleviate some of the immediate frustrations of the Operations Managers and build my credibility. My second goal was to under stand the reasons for the delay. My third goal was to reduce the time needed to fill the positions.

To achieve my first goal, I met with the various Operations Mangers to understand their concerns, needs and desires. I then told them about my plan and reassured them I'd meet their needs soon. To maintain and build on this new trust and credibility, I also kept them up to date on my progress. To achieve my second goal I studied the organization's recruitment process, analyzed competency profiles and job descriptions. By doing this, I also found a way to achieve my third goal. In my analysis of the situation, I realized that it was taking a long time to fill the positions because these positions were not fully advertised. Moreover, candidates who were screened first by the recruiter were not immediately referred to the Operations Managers for second interviews. The delay could be a week, and some candidates had interviewed and accepted positions from other companies.

To increase exposure to these vacant positions, I found places where I could advertise for little to no cost. I also contacted universities to send out an e-mail about these job opportunities to their alumni who had studied in a related field. I also reviewed résumés that were previously received to find potential candidates in the pile. To speed up the interview process, I convinced the Operations Managers to be available (where possible) 45 min-utes after the start of my interviews with candidates. This enabled me to refer good candidates immediately to the second interview, cutting the wait gap between the first and second interview! Some Managers preferred being a part of my interview instead of waiting because they wouldn't know if they would be needed for a second interview. I was fine with that as either way, the process to getting the stronger candidates hired would be shortened.

R 4 of the 5 vacancies were filled within one month's time and this represented a 15% decline in the time it took to hire. This was a significant achievement considering that I never did this before. My reward was a contract extension.

Analysis

This is an exceptional answer because the individual achieved great results in spite of her lack of experience. She acted with a sense of urgency and proactively mapped out a plan and executed with great diligence. The individual analyzed existing processes to find ways of improving them. She focused on her desired end result of reducing the hiring time and didn't let different preferred styles of doing that become an obstacle.

5. **How to get from Strong to Stronger:**

▸ Show that you had a *clear plan* to achieve your desired outcome

▸ Show that you *persevered* in face of adversity

▸ Show that you made *personal sacrifices or took risks*

▶ **Learning**

1. Recognizes areas of personal strength and areas of development opportunity. Takes steps to build on expertise through self development and the acquisition of new knowledge.

2. Skill Level	Description
WEAK	▸ Views learning as a passive rather than active exercise ▸ Shows no curiosity to learn new approaches or knowledge ▸ Has acquired basic knowledge through coursework only ▸ Willing to participate in planned learning sessions ▸ Usually behind on trends ▸ Uncomfortable working in areas different from experiences
STRONG	▸ Actively pursues learning and development opportunities to achieve results and contribute to continuous improvements ▸ Reflects on performance, both successes and failures, to see how things could have been done differently for better results ▸ Proactively identifies new ways of doing things and learning plans ▸ Seeks feedback on performance and incorporates into improvement
EXCEPTIONAL	▸ Takes steps to maintain an in-depth knowledge of area of expertise ▸ Proactively seek others' ideas and perspectives and integrates learnings ▸ Pursues learning beyond current job or identified needs ▸ Anticipates future needs and proactively prepares to meet them ▸ Takes ownership of own professional development ▸ Focuses development in areas of greatest value ▸ Stays current in a demanding and changing environment ▸ Proactively develops others and coaches peers

3. **Various ways of asking the question:**

Tell me about a time when you...
- ▸ learned something totally new and how you applied what you learned
- ▸ made a mistake and what you would do differently if you had to do it over again
- ▸ took charge of your own development to improve your performance on the job

"Tell me about a time when you learned something totally new and how you applied what you learned?"

4. **Weak Answer:**

One of the recent marketing courses I took required me to design a survey and customize a statistical analysis program to read and run the survey results . This was my first time using the program and so I had to take a few introductory courses offered by the University to learn the basics of the program. Since this assignment was due within 2 weeks, I choose to focus only on aspects of the program I needed. In the end, my ability to learn quickly enabled me to use the program effectively and obtain an A on the report.

Analysis

Although the learning may have been significant, the individual sought to learn a new statistical program that was a mandatory part of her course. This example was also weak because the individual only focused on learning the basic parts of the program.

Strong Answer:

B In my program of study, courses are highly theoretical and no courses offered practical hands on experience or knowledge that could be used in workforce. Recognizing this, I initiated a skills and knowledge exchange forum between my classmates. This program required students to volunteer their time teaching other students the skills they acquired in their past. I first sent out an e-mail asking for volunteers but no one came forward. I reasoned that this was because I had sent the e-mail during the winter holidays and the message was not personally addressed.

A Instead of resending the e-mail, I approached some of the students and asked them to volunteer. These students all said they would attend the work-shops but did not want to administer them. They felt that they did not have anything valuable to contribute nor did they have time. I realized that this was a problem and so I adapted quickly. I knew that my approach had to change and my message to the students had to be more convincing.

I looked up individual student résumés and approached the individuals who I felt had key skills that interested a majority of students. I convinced them that they only had to prepare for their presentation while I handled all of the logistics. I also told them that in exchange, they would receive feedback on their presentation skills and add this experience on their résumé.

R Because of my desire to get practical insight to compliment my theoretical courses, I initiated and created a learning forum that not only allowed me to learn, it enabled additional learning for all my classmates. By pursuing this endeavour, I also learned that my initial approach to get volunteers was not personal enough and that I did not fully understand the students' needs or concerns before I sent out the email. I applied my learning by customizing my approach as well as targeting a few key students. By doing that I was able to convince two individuals to put on a joint workshop which benefited everyone.

Analysis

The individual proactively pursued new learning which improved insight for everyone. She learned from her own unsuccessful actions and adjusted her approach to achieve better results. She also understood the importance of getting feedback for the presenters so that they could also develop their own presentation skills.

Exceptional Answer:

B In my program of study, courses are highly theoretical and there were no courses that offered practical hands on experience or knowledge that could be used in workforce. At the same time, I noticed that many students in the program had very diverse work experiences and yet there was an untapped opportunity to exchange this knowledge. Seeing a need, I came up with the idea to create the Knowledge and Skills Exchange Forum where students could teach and learn from each other skills that were not taught in the program. This forum would allow the students from my Program to stay current and be competitive in the job market.

A I discussed the idea with students in my program. I wanted to find out if others would support this idea and get their input about the content of the Knowledge and Exchange Forum. Everyone I spoke to was very enthusiastic about the idea and in my discussions I gathered a list of key areas where the Program had knowledge gaps. I then analyzed the list and got feedback as to which areas were of greatest value and pursued these opportunities first. In addition, I also had to consult the Faculty and Administration. In my sales pitch, I emphasized how this would be a student-run initiative that would complement courses offered in the Program and help students stay current and competitive. I asked for support to run it once as a test, and if it was successful, it could continue yearly as an enhancement to the program. Furthermore, the process ensured students would get the latest learning each year as the facilitators were always students from the class with their most recent experiences. With support from the students and Faculty and Administration, I spearheaded the forum. I created flyers highlighting the premise of the Forum and encouraged students to volunteer.

R I got two students to volunteer as speakers and we held a workshop on the students' area of expertise. 80% of students participated. Students from all levels attended the workshop. The feedback received was tremendous and the skill and knowledge program remains today an integral part of the program.

Analysis

This example took the strong one step further in two ways: 1. The individual analyzed a list of key learning opportunities and focused on the areas of greatest opportunity. 2. The individual considered how this learning opportunity could be kept current in a changing environment. By doing so, she demonstrated the ability to anticipate future needs and help the faculty prepare to meet them.

5. **How to get from Strong to Stronger:**

▸ Show you *sought feedback, new ideas or different perspectives from others*

▸ Show you *learned from your mistakes*

▸ Show you *empowered and enabled yourself and/or others to take responsibility for personal learning*

▶ **Flexibility**

1. Is open to change and new information. Adapts behaviour and work methods in response to new information, changing conditions or unexpected obstacles. Adjusts and can work effectively within a variety of situations and with diverse individuals or groups.

2. Skill Level	Description
WEAK	▸ Listens to others' viewpoints but silently retains one's own ▸ Always follows procedures ▸ May be reluctant to try something new ▸ Critical of others actions and do not accept others differences
STRONG	▸ Willingly tries new things and compromises ▸ Decides what to do based on the circumstances of the situation ▸ Change own approach to adapt to others' responses while maintaining one's own needs
EXCEPTIONAL	▸ Effectively works in different environments, cultures, locations, technologies or various types of people ▸ Open to new ideas, circumstances and information ▸ Accepts others, and embraces differences ▸ Shifts focus and activities quickly in response to changing priorities, unexpected obstacles, new demands or tasks

3. **Various ways of asking the question:**

Tell me about a time when you...
  ▸ were open-minded about an opinion that was different from yours
  ▸ adjusted quickly to changes over which you had no control
  ▸ adjusted to a colleague's working style in order to achieve team objectives
  ▸ were given new information that affected a decision you already made

"Tell me about a time when you adjusted quickly to changes over which you had no control?"

4. Weak Answer:

I had agreed to design a web page for a friend who was going to start her own business. She offered to pay me because professionals charged more, and as a student, I needed the extra money. She had decided on a web host, and knowing that, I started planning how the site was to be designed. A couple weeks later, she changed her mind and decided to use another web host company. I thought her previous decision was better, but she still wanted to go with her new decision. Since this was her company, I really couldn't control which choice she made. I had to re-think my plan for her web site because the services and package with the new web hosting company was different from the previous one. I had a deadline to finish the website by and this was complicated by the fact that I had to change my plan. Also, the second company she chose offered less website building tools meaning I had to find other sources of software tools which I had to then learn how to use. Nonetheless, I finished it on time and she was happy with the result.

Analysis

The individual did not embrace the change, but rather, had to "deal" with it. She thinks she was flexible because something outside of her control changed, however, you can sense that if she had a choice, she would not have made this change. Being truly flexible includes seeing the benefits of a change, embracing it and proactively bringing out wins with the change.

Strong Answer:

B I was hired by a local newspaper to help them create new business via classifieds and advertisements. They hired me because they liked my innovative skills and wanted me to come up with new ways to grow sales. I was very excited to impact strategy so before starting the job I did some research and had a few ideas on how to pursue new opportunities. However, my first day on the job, I was told they needed me to replace a former Account Manager who had quit and who had many customers switch to competitors. Instead of creating programs, I had to sell. This was a situation beyond my control and I had to adapt quite quickly.

A I took the time to speak to each customer who had left. I asked questions regarding what they liked and didn't like what it would take to bring them back. They usually asked for things we basically did not offer at that time. In this circumstance, I actually used the innovative skills I was originally hired for to build some new package offerings. While doing this, I asked my colleagues for any feedback their customers gave and adjusted my ideas accordingly. To accommodate most customers' needs, I created a customizable program where each account handler had the opportunity to offer different incentives to different customers as long as the total value was within a certain range. I proposed these ideas to my manager and got support to actually implement some of them.

R In the end, I was able bring back some old customers as well as find new ones with the new packages. The packages I created were deployed throughout the organization and it helped boost company sales by about 5% that year.

Analysis

The example was strong because the individual was willing to try something new and compromise. She considered her circumstance and chose a focus that met both parties needs partway. She proactively sought others feed back and reflected her openness to their input by adjusting her ideas accordingly.

Exceptional Answer:

B I was hired by a local newspaper to help them create new business via classifieds and advertisements. They hired me because they liked my innovative skills and wanted me to come up with new ways to grow sales. I was very excited to impact strategy so before starting the job I did some research and had a few ideas on how to pursue new opportunities. However, my first day on the job, I was told they needed me to replace a former Account Manager who had quit and who had many customers switch to competitors. Instead of creating programs, I had to sell. This was a situation beyond my control and I had to adapt quite quickly.

A I embraced this challenge and took the time to speak to each current and past customers. I wanted to make sure none of the current ones left while finding ways to bring back the old ones. I asked questions regarding what they liked and didn't like. I asked customers that left what it would take to bring them back and I asked existing customers what were their key unmet needs.

Most of the existing customers simply wanted to continue to receive good service and feel valued. So to make sure they felt that way, I sent an apology letter if they had indicated unsatisfactory service and I sent a thank you letter to everyone else. I included small bonus incentives which offered discounts or multiple-purchase offers to give customers value as well as get additional sales for us.

Customers that left usually asked for things we basically did not offer at that time. In this circumstance, I actually used the innovative skills I was originally hired for to build some new package offerings. While doing this, I asked my colleagues for any feedbacks their customers gave and adjusted my ideas accordingly. To accommodate most customers' needs, I created a customizable program where each account handler had the opportunity to offer different incentives to different customers as long as the total value was within a certain range. I proposed these ideas to my manager and got support to actually implement some of them.

R In the end, I was able to almost eliminate customer turnover. I was also able to bring back some old customers and find new ones with the new packages. The packages I created were deployed throughout the organization and it helped boost company sales by about 5% that year.

Analysis

This answer is exceptional because the individual embraced the change and created winning results with it. She not only continued to use her creative skills, she accepted her new role entirely by ensuring existing customer stayed. She shifted her focus quickly from solely creating to include selling and found a way to leverage both together. She was open to new ideas and feedback and accepted differences by creating a program that met various needs.

5. How to get from Strong to Stronger:

▸ Show that you *were creative in responding to the unexpected situation*

▸ Show that you *readjusted your priorities or changed your thinking in an unexpected situation*

▸ Show that you *performed under pressure*

Interview
Questions & Answers

HOLISTIC

Interview Questions & Answers — Holistic

In this section, we provide you with examples of typical answers and answers with an edge because unlike behavioural questions, holistic questions are usually not rated on a scale. Holistic questions are used to understand your overall character, work habits and fit with the organization as well as uncover anything about you that may not be ideal. If you perform well in the behavioural section of the interview, don't stress the holistic questions; just make sure your answers leave a positive impression. Below is a list of the 11 most common types of holistic questions:

11 Most Common Types of Holistic Questions

▸ Résumé	▸ Interest	▸ Hypothetical/Case Study
▸ Fit	▸ Strengths/Weaknesses	▸ Work Pattern
▸ Well Roundedness	▸ Drive	▸ Attitude
▸ Watch Outs	▸ Long Term Goals	

For each type of holistic question we will give you:

1. an overview of what interviewers are looking for

2. examples of how each type of holistic question could be asked

3. examples and analyses of typical answers and answers with an edge

4. tips to strengthen your response

INTERVIEW TIP

Remember three tips while answering Holistic questions:

1. Convert question into a behavioural question.
2. Choose competency carefully.
3. Keep it short.

▶ **Résumé**

1. Some résumés tend to embellish the candidate's work experience. Knowing this, interviewers ask résumé questions to get you to elaborate or clarify items on your résumé to determine if you really did what you said you did. When résumé questions are asked, the interviewer is looking to…

    > ▶ Validate your résumé
    > ▶ Gain insight into strong competency skills
    > ▶ Gain insight into indicated areas of interest

2. **Various ways of asking the question:**

    ▶ Tell me more about this experience
    ▶ So I see you have an interest in "x"?
    ▶ You said you lead this project; tell me how you did that?

    ### *"Tell me about your last summer position at the bank?"*

3. **Typical Answer:**

I was a Customer Service Representative and my primary responsibility was to help my customers complete transactions quickly and accurately while making sure they were happy with the service.

Analysis

The answer is a very brief role description. The individual had an opportunity to demonstrate her exceptional skills in a particular competency and did not! Achievements in this role were also not highlighted.

Answer with an Edge:

B As a Customer Service Representative, my primary responsibility was to help customers' complete transactions quickly and accurately while making sure they were happy with the service. Usually the busiest time was just before a long weekend. It wouldn't be unusual to get a frustrated customer because of the long wait in line.

A I wanted to make sure every customer was happy. When I sensed a frustrated customer I would try to quickly diffuse the frustration. I would apologize for the long wait and make sure my manner was pleasant so they wouldn't feel like "just another customer". I would use their name to reassure them that we remembered them and valued their business. I would also try to build personalized service. For example, if they were exchanging for foreign currency, I'd generally ask if they were going on a trip. That way, they'd hopefully be talking about something they were looking forward to, and it'd leave me something to ask them about next time I saw them again. Our team has regular meetings to discuss how to minimize customer frustrations and I would regularly provided my recommendations.

R I've been recognized several times for my customer service skills including one where a customer wrote a letter to my branch to recognize me and another time for exceeding quotas for successful referrals of customers to our RRSP department.

Analysis

This answer is much better than the previous one because it highlights a specific competency and demonstrates the action taken to achieve great results. In this example, the individual also demonstrates a desire for continuous improvement for herself and the organization.

4. **How to Improve an Average Answer**

▸ Highlight a relevant competency

▸ Personalize your answer to go beyond a job description

▶ **Fit**

1. How you will fit in with the company's culture, your personality and how you will get along with your team and manager are important to the interviewer. The interviewer is trying to learn more about you beyond the skills you possess. When fit questions are asked, the interviewer is looking to determine whether…

   ▸ You will thrive in the company's corporate culture
   ▸ You have similar principles and values as the company
   ▸ Your style of work and underlying motivation match the company incentives

2. **Various ways of asking the question:**

   ▸ Describe the type of environment you want to work in
   ▸ What did you like best about "x" experience?
   ▸ What was your favourite job and why?

   ### *"What was your favourite job and why?"*

3. **Typical Answer:**

My favourite job was one where I had the opportunity to use my creativity skills to plan and implement recreational activities for seniors. It was fun, I enjoyed the responsibility and it felt good to give the seniors something that would make them happy.

Analysis

While the answer touches on a few possible competencies (leadership, problem-solving) it doesn't expand to describe how effectively the skills were used. It also doesn't highlight any significant results or highlight how the individual's interests and skills will fit with the position in question.

Answer with an Edge:

B My favourite job so far was when I was a Customer Service Representative at the bank.

A I liked this job because I enjoyed working with external customers. The position also allowed me to challenge myself to find solutions to problems independently.

R I got some of the best results in terms of exceeding quotas, getting high customer service evaluations and doing it quickly. This is also why I'd like this position at your call center because I believe the atmosphere is similar and I would do well in it.

Analysis

This example illustrates that you can use the same experience, change the wording and have it targeted toward a completely different question. This answer highlights competencies that are relevant to the position you are applying for.

4. **How to Improve an Average Answer**

▸ Ensure aspects of your favourite job _are_ evident in the job you are applying for

▸ Ensure aspects of your least favourite job are _not_ evident in the job you are applying for

▶ **Well Roundedness**

1. Many interviewers also look for strong extra-curricular involvement or interests outside of work and academic. These experiences not only highlight certain competencies, they demonstrate that you are someone who enjoys life. A well-rounded individual may also be perceived as someone able to help enhance the company atmosphere. These types of questions also lighten the mood and provide interesting insights into your character. When well roundness questions are asked, the interviewer is looking to determine whether...

> ▸ You can balance a heavy workload and personal life
> ▸ Your involvement in the community/volunteer work is real and not solely for display on your résumé
> ▸ You have interests outside of school/work

2. **Various ways of asking the question:**

   ▸ What do you like to do outside of school/work?
   ▸ Tell me about your involvement in a school organization.
   ▸ Describe your interests.

"Describe your interests?"

3. **Typical Answer:**

I play a lot of sports. I'm part of a basketball league and a volleyball league. I also love travelling; I've been to Europe and Asia and I'd like to do more.

Analysis

The response is very common and does not make the individual stand out. It also is just a list that provides little insights about you.

Answer with an Edge:

B I enjoy playing team sports. At least once a week, I am out in the basketball court shooting hoops.

A I've been captain of the same basketball team for the last five years. I like sports because its both physically and mentally demanding. You need to anticipate your opponents play and counter it. There is a lot of problem-solving involved in this.

R Last year, my team participated in an annual tournament and we won our first championship! I am really proud of this achievement. As a reward for our-selves, the team back-packed through Europe. We hit countless landmarks and got through 15 countries in 3 months. I think the most expensive part was when we came back and had to develop about 50 roles of film each!

Analysis

The example not only highlights the individual's interest but also shows that she has leadership qualities and the desire to explore and learn new things. The individual also appears very passionate about her interests, which suggest that this passion could be translated to the job.

4. How to Improve an Average Answer

▸ Tell a funny story

▸ Explain _why_ you do what you do — why you enjoy it

▶ **Watch-Outs**

1. In addition to finding reasons to hire you, interviewers also try to find reasons why they should not hire you. Watch out questions are designed to find out negative aspects about you or information that would not make you an ideal fit for the job. They highlight red flags. Interviewers are on the look out for negative patterns in your work history. When watch out questions are asked, the interviewer is looking to determine whether you…

    > ▶ Have been fired before and why
    > ▶ Work well with others and get along well with your past bosses
    > ▶ Have bad work habits
    > ▶ Can be promoted

2. **Various ways of asking the question:**

    ▶ What was your least favourite job and why?
    ▶ Why did you leave your most current position?
    ▶ Are you interested in working for the company where you held a summer position? If not, why not?

    ### *"What was your least favourite job and why?"*

3. **Typical Answer:**

My least favourite job was when I worked at a call center. My role was to handle customer telephone and e-mail complaints. I didn't like it because it was a very negative environment and the job was very tedious. I like a more positive atmosphere where I have lots of responsibilities and variety of tasks.

Analysis

The reasons listed for not liking the job is satisfactory. No one likes a negative environment and the fact that the individual prefers more responsibilities is good. However, in any job and at any company, there will always be negative people, and some tasks are bound to be tedious, especially if you are applying for an entry level position. To stand out, you need to give an answer that conflicts the least with the job you are interviewing for and one that does not contain common elements of what most people would say they do not like.

Answer with an Edge:

B My least favourite job is actually not on my résumé. It was when I was still in high school and worked as a part-time receptionist for my parent's Real Estate company. This was during one of my summers.

A It wasn't because the job was bad; in fact I had a lot of responsibilities and I learned a lot because some days I had to work by myself. However, I didn't like was the fact that I was working for my parents. I wanted to feel like I earned the job by myself. This was my least favourite job because it gave me the least sense of self-accomplishment. I didn't feel like I earned the position, I felt like I was "handed it".

R Nonetheless, it was a great opportunity. It gave me the chance to gain some good experience and demonstrate some strong skills at a young age. This experience helped me get another job on my own the next summer!

Analysis

This example was not evident on the individual's résumé and this provided new and unexpected information to the interviewer. The key element that makes this answer stand out was that the response placed a positive spin on the experience. It also demonstrates that the individual likes to make things happen and rely on her own skills rather than on other people's influences.

4. How to Improve an Average Answer

‣ Ensure the element you considered unfavourable in your previous positions is not a key component of the job you are applying

‣ Ensure you do not present yourself negatively for any competency

‣ End with something positive

▶ # Interest

1. Interest refers to interest in the organization or role. Interviewers ask what you know about the organization to gage your interest level in the organization or position. Sometimes, interviewers may also be assessing where their company stacks up against other companies you have applied to. Interviewers are also afraid you may leave the company soon after being hired. They spend thousands on recruiting and training so they want to make sure they are hiring someone who will stay. When company interest questions are asked, the interviewer is looking to determine whether you...

    ▸ Are proactive in researching the company in advance
    ▸ Agree with the company's mission and values
    ▸ Have a sincere interest for the company

2. **Various ways of asking the question:**

    ▸ What do you know about our company?
    ▸ Why do you want to work for our company?
    ▸ Why do you want this position?

    ### *"Why do you want to work for our company?"*

3. **Typical Answer:**

You're one of the biggest companies in the industry and one of the best in terms of coming out with innovative new products and I'd like to be a part of all that. I also learned from your web-site and information session that you have a lot of training for your employees. I think I'd be able to learn a lot and develop here.

Analysis

This response shows some evidence that the individual researched the organization. However, this response is weak because it focuses only on what the individual could get from the organization and not what she could contribute.

Answer with an Edge:

B You've been rated as one of the best companies to work for, partly because of your leadership in the industry, and also because of how well you treat your people. Both those things are important to me.

A One of the main reasons I'd like to work here is that unlike most companies, you entrust your new hires with meaningful positions from the start. The website testimonies from your employees really convinced me that this is true. More than that, your organization gives back to the community in the form of a volunteer program where employees could contribute to the community on work hours. You also set up new employees with a Mentor. This would provide me with the inspiration and tools to contribute to the organization. I could also help the community and hence help enhance the organization's image while fulfilling a personal desire to contribute.

R I'd really like the opportunity to work in an environment where everyone strives to do their best, and I think it's an environment where I'd excel.

Analysis

The individual demonstrated sincere interest in the organization because she had specific reasons for wanting to work there. She also matched her values to the organizational values. The individual also demonstrated how she could contribute to the organization.

4. How to Improve an Average Answer

▸ Indicate that you have researched the organization or position

▸ Align your values to the organization's values

▶ Strengths/Weaknesses

1. Strength/Weakness questions help the interviewer determine how you view yourself. Your response provides insights on your ability to be reflective. It also helps the interviewer determine if you are modest or boastful. When strength/weakness questions are asked, the interviewer is looking to determine whether...

> ▸ Your weaknesses will inhibit you from succeeding in the position
> ▸ Your strengths will lead you to succeed in the position
> ▸ You are realistic in your self-assessment

2. **Various ways of asking the question:**

> ▸ What's the greatest asset you'd bring to our organization?
> ▸ Where would you say you need improvement?
> ▸ What kind of training do you think you'll need?

"Where would you say you need improvement?"

3. **Typical Answer:**

I'm a perfectionist and sometimes that means I spend too much time working on something. I want everything "just right"...I guess I'm too detailed-oriented. I need to spend less time on the things that aren't as important.

Analysis

Interviewers probably hear this answer 90% of the time they ask this question! In the interviewer's mind we're thinking, "Ok, this is the rehearsed answer..." Pick an example of an area that you had recently improved upon.

Answer with an Edge:

B I have a tendency to be a control freak. In teams, I like to be the person who does the editing and the delegating of tasks. I realize that sometimes I may be double and triple checking someone's work and this may upset others because they may feel I don't trust them.

A I am learning to trust my team. I now try to listen first and talk later. I also involve others in the distribution of work and actively seek input for new ideas. Sometimes, I also communicate this weakness upfront so that if I do appear controlling, people won't take offence and would feel comfortable pointing this out to me.

R So far it is working. Not only is teamwork less stressful for me, but I also feel that I respect my team more and in turn they also respect and trust me too.

Analysis

This answer demonstrates that the individual is introspective. She is honest about her shortcomings and is very aware of the impact of her weakness on others. She has also identified ways to overcome this weakness.

4. How to Improve an Average Answer

▸ Ensure that your example for a weakness is NOT one of the skills they are looking for

▸ Demonstrate how you have improved

▸ Do not say you are a perfectionist

▶ **Drive**

1. Your underlying motivation to succeed is important to an interviewer because it is assumed that if you want to personally do well, you will also likely help the organization progress. Interviewers are usually looking for people who will do more than just what is minimally required. When questions about your drive are asked, the interviewer is looking to determine whether you…

  ▶ Are self-motivated and want to succeed
  ▶ Would set stretch targets
  ▶ Have a positively competitive mind-set
  ▶ Desire career advancement

2. **Various ways of asking the question:**

  ▶ What motivates you?
  ▶ How would you define success?
  ▶ Where do you see yourself five years from now?

"How would you define success?"

3. **Typical Answer:**

In the context of achievement, success to me means achieving my goals. However, if I aim for a goal and did everything I could to achieve that goal but don't reach it because of other uncontrollable factors, then I still consider myself successful.

Analysis

The answer demonstrates a positive perspective which is good. However, it also appears that the individual may be complacent with average results. The individual indicated that she will try her best, but this statement is not specific.

Answer with an Edge:

B Success to me would mean meeting or exceeding my goals. My personal goals are to always try to make a difference, bring about positive change and constantly learn. If I am able to do this, I'd consider myself successful. I like to set targets for everything I do. These targets include minimum goals (minimum standard that I would accept) and stretch goals (difficult to reach but possible if I am persistent).

A For example, at school, I must have a minimum of 80% on all my courses. However, I always aim to get 90+%. Depending on the course, to get the 90+% would mean I'd have to deliver something beyond what the professor expects. I would ask the professor what would meet this standard.

R This system works for me because by always aiming to exceed my goals, I'm almost always certain to hit it.

Analysis

This answer demonstrates personal drive because the individual actually thought about what success means. An individual who wants to make a difference would likely seek ways to bring the position to a more effective level.

4. How to Improve an Average Answer

▸ Use an example where you've accomplished something even though others said it was impossible

▸ Show you will not accept failure, but instead will find a way to overcome your obstacles.

▶ **Long Term Goals**

1. Interviewers want to know your long term goals to determine if the job you are applying for is a step towards this future! If it is not, you would likely under perform in the job and/or leave. Your departure will cost the organization additional time and money to recruit and train. Interviewers are looking out for their best interest if they consider yours as well. When questions about your long-term goals are asked, the interviewer is determining whether...

    ▸ You have realistic long term goals
    ▸ The position is aligned with where you can and want to progress with the company
    ▸ You will or will not leave the company soon after being hired

2. **Various ways of asking the question:**

    ▸ Where do you see yourself five years from now?
    ▸ If you got this position, what would you like your next position to be?
    ▸ How long do you see yourself staying in this position?

    "Where do you see yourself five years from now?"

3. **Typical Answer:**

I think I'd still be learning a lot five years from now. I think I would have learned a lot, and I'd like to do more challenging work. I'd like to have progressed to the next level beyond this one.

Analysis

This answer demonstrates a desire to continuously learn and progress which is good. However, it doesn't demonstrate that you've thought through your goals, and wanting to progress is very vague and extremely common.

Answer with an Edge:

B In five years, I would like to be in a position of greater responsibilities while at the same time entrusting upon a team with the detail work. This means I would spend more time on issues of strategic importance to the organization as well as spend time developing and motivating my team to succeed.

A To get there, I need to learn quickly, focus and bring strong results to my first position. I need to do this to establish credibility so that others would trust me to lead, train and guide them. When I have my team, I would need to energize them to achieve strong results with me, break down their barriers and keep them focused.

R This would then position me competitively for a leadership position as described previously.

Analysis

The individual demonstrates insight into how promotions may occur in the organization. She sets out a plan that is not only realistic but it is also very specific. The long term plan also represents a higher need to develop others not just herself. This example is solidifying the individual as a good long-term investment.

4. How to Improve an Average Answer

▸ Ensure that your long term goal is specific and realistic and makes senses with the job you are applying to

▸ Align your response to how the organization promotes its employees

▶ # **Hypothetical/Case Study**

1. Hypothetical or case study questions help the interviewer determine how you think and how you would react and act in unfamiliar situations. The hypothetical or case study questions could be difficult because of people's natural tendency to jump into the action, without thinking about the situation in its entirety. To avoid this, listen first, summarize the case given and ask for clarification. When hypothetical or case study questions are asked, the interviewer is looking to determine whether you…

   ▸ Could think quickly
   ▸ Could perform well in unfamiliar situations
   ▸ Possess logic and reasoning
   ▸ Could handle pressure

2. **Various ways of asking the question:**

   ▸ What would you do if…?
   ▸ How would you handle this situation?
   ▸ How would you manager of a team where everyone had different goals?

   ### *"How would you manage a team where several of the people are older than you?"*

3. **Typical Answer:**

I would frequently ask for their input to demonstrate I value their experience and respect them.

Analysis

This example illustrates the common tendency to say, "I would do c because of d." This example jumps right into describing the action and justifying them. The reasoning and results of the action are not evident. **Use BAR!**

Answer with an Edge:

B If I were the leader of this team, my goal would be to have us achieve some thing significant together, like exceeding our sales target by 15%.

A To do this, I would motivate my team and align the necessary resources and support. If several of my team members are older than me, I would anticipate that there might be some resistance towards a younger manager who's new to the company. I would want to make sure that whatever actions I took would not make anyone on the team feel like certain people are being treated differently because of their age. Instead of jumping in and imposing a stretch target on my team, I would have one-to-one first meetings. This would give us a chance to get to know one another better and encourage them to find opportunities for improvement. If any of the older team members felt that a younger manager would be inexperienced, I would position this as a chance for them to help me understand the situation, their needs.

R These types of discussions would help me align my team towards a common goal. Getting to know each individual member at the beginning would help me know how to motivate them and in return this will help them feel valued and respected. The meetings would also allow me to learn about the obstacles the team is facing and find solutions to achieving better results.

Analysis

This hypothetical case study leaves it open for one to choose the competency to highlight. The individual could choose to illustrate strong communication or team skills. This answer also demonstrates that the individual has leader-ship qualities.

4. How to Improve an Average Answer

▸ Highlight strengths in multiple competencies

▸ Give an example of a similar situation you faced and achieved strong results

▶ **Work Pattern**

1. Your work habits determine if the work assigned will get done. Being hard working is a good trait to have because this is interpreted to mean you will be accountable for what you do. When work pattern questions are asked, the interviewer is looking to determine whether you…

   ▸ Consistently meet deadlines
   ▸ Are reliable
   ▸ Would do what it takes to get the work done

2. **Various ways of asking the question:**

   ▸ How do you balance your work life schedule?
   ▸ Describe your work style
   ▸ What is your philosophy on working long hours?

   ### *"How do you balance your work life schedule?"*

3. **Typical Answer:**

My work is very important to me and I will devote a lot of time to make sure I do it well. I'll still spend time with my family and friends, but I will make sure my work gets done first. Of course, if there are family emergencies, that would take priority.

Analysis

This response is vague and does not provide any insights on your work habits. There is no evidence that the individual is a hard worker.

Answer with an Edge:

B Overall, family is very important to me and will always be my number one priority. I also think it's important to have time to rejuvenate and stay fresh and well-rounded so that I continue to be efficient at work. That being said, my career is also very important to me at this point.

A I believe I'm at a stage in my life where I have the time and the energy to push myself to excel. I would likely spend a lot of time in my work in order to bring significant results to my job and career.

R This is the same way of thinking that I've applied to my studies, and my grades are very good. I believe this demonstrates that I will be able to handle both a heavy work load, deliver strong results, and still have time for my personal life.

Analysis

The answer demonstrates confidence and ability to succeed. The individual knows her priorities and appears to be handling them well. She can see the bigger picture and also know when and where to focus her efforts. She will likely not overwork and get burnt out. Using a past example, she demonstrates credibility and evidence of bringing strong results. This answer also highlights a philosophy towards work.

4. How to Improve an Average Answer

▸ Use a real life example to add credibility

▸ Give some reasoning: why do you think the way you think?

▸ Present a situation where you had to multi-task

▶ **Attitude**

1. Having a positive attitude is important to fostering a good and healthy workplace environment. Positive attitudes strengthen team relationships and leads to greater work productivity; in contrast, negative attitudes make the workplace undesirable and stressful. When attitude questions are asked, the interviewer is looking to determine whether you…

> ▸ Would contribute to a positive work environment
> ▸ Would persevere even in stressful situations
> ▸ Are willing to share and help others

2. **Various ways of asking the question:**

> ▸ How would your friends describe you?
> ▸ How would you describe yourself?
> ▸ What motto do you live by?

"Use three words to tell me how your friends would describe you?"

3. **Typical Answer:**

"Easy-going", "Active" because I like to play sports and do outdoor stuff and "Silly".

Analysis

These words indicate the individual would probably be easy to work with, however, this response does not reinforce a competency.

Answer with an Edge:

B They'd probably say I'm "Inclusive", "Funny" and "Driven"

A "Inclusive" probably because I'm always organizing events and get-togethers and it's always the more the merrier and we have a ton of fun. "Funny" probably because we're always laughing and that's just what I hear them say about me. And "Driven" probably because they see how devoted I am to the work that I do in my summer jobs, extra-curricular activities and studies.

R I'm always pushing myself to the next level achievement, so if you put it all together, you get really big, funny parties where there's always a new theme!

Analysis

Each attribute is backed up by examples. In fact, the attribute also highlight underlying desirable traits such as well-roundedness (participation in activities outside of school), positive attitude (making other smile), and leadership (ability to organize events).

4. How to Improve an Average Answer

▸ Include elements about your character from different perspectives and activities

▸ Back up attributes with examples

You are now armed with two key resources to improving your interview skills — you know how to answer questions (BAR) and you know what the interviewer will likely be looking for because you understand the two main types of interview questions. Apply this knowledge by thinking of your answers and practice out loud. To help you increase your chances of getting hired, the next section presents you with tips on what you should not and should do to help make the interview result in a job offer!

Avoid Mistakes Candidates Make

**Avoid mistakes
you could easily correct,
let us show you how!**

Avoid Mistakes Candidates Make

More times than you may think we have watched potentially good candidates walk out without a job offer because they made mistakes that made them *appear* unqualified. Avoid mistakes that you could *easily* correct, let us show you how:

▶ Mistake #1: Not knowing how to use the job ad to anticipate questions

When people have interviews, usually they just sit and wonder what the interviewer may ask. Those who put in more effort would pick up an interview book and memorize 101 most common interview questions. Then they wonder how they would answer the question. Stop wondering! Stop memorizing 101 questions! In fact most interviews are very predictable. You can discover in advance the majority of questions that will likely be asked of you.

Strategy: Use the Job Advertisement to Predict Questions

You have a secret weapon right in front of you! The job advertisement will help you identify the competencies required for the job. Think of the job ad as the organization's cry for help and in this cry, the organization will put their wish list for an ideal candidate. Since competencies determine one's success in a job, these competencies would likely be included in the job advertisement. Some organizations clearly state and list the competencies; others embed them within the job advertisement. To anticipate questions using the job advertisement, follow these steps:

1. *Read the job ad and categorize elements in the advertisement according to "Behaviours", "Competencies", and "Other"*
   - ▸ Behaviours begin with a verb (they tend to be the definition of a competency)
   - ▸ Competencies may be labelled or are one word adjectives
   - ▸ Other is anything that does not fit in either categories above

2. *Match the behaviours and competencies to each other*
3. *Look at the list of possible questions in this book and write down all the questions that could be asked for each competency identified*
4. *Items in the "Other" category are topics that may come up during the interview. Be prepared to discuss your abilities in these areas also.*

Let us show you with an actual job advertisement:

Step 1: Read the job ad and categorize elements in the advertisement according to "Behaviours", "Competencies", and "Other"

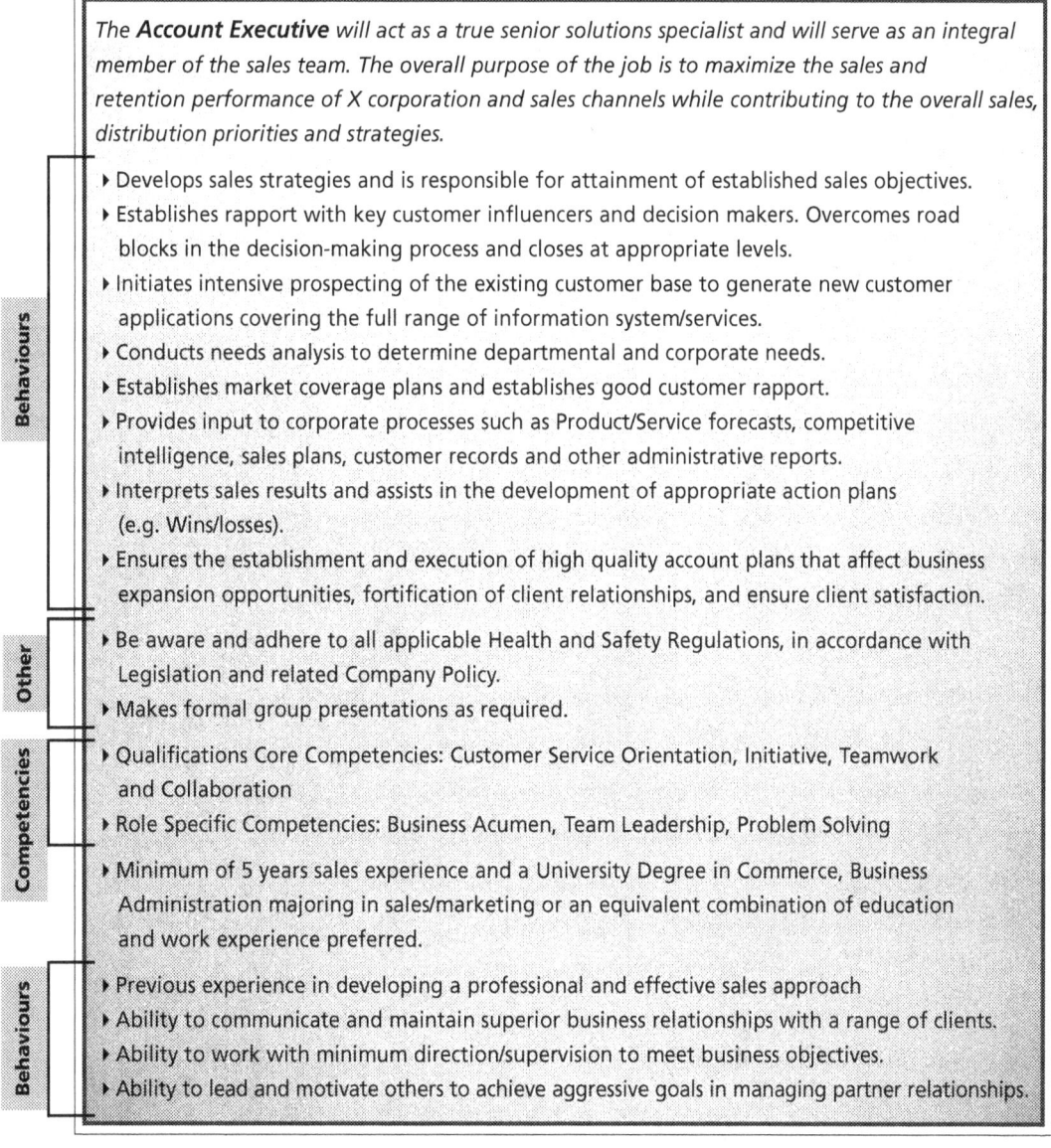

The **Account Executive** will act as a true senior solutions specialist and will serve as an integral member of the sales team. The overall purpose of the job is to maximize the sales and retention performance of X corporation and sales channels while contributing to the overall sales, distribution priorities and strategies.

Behaviours
▸ Develops sales strategies and is responsible for attainment of established sales objectives.
▸ Establishes rapport with key customer influencers and decision makers. Overcomes road blocks in the decision-making process and closes at appropriate levels.
▸ Initiates intensive prospecting of the existing customer base to generate new customer applications covering the full range of information system/services.
▸ Conducts needs analysis to determine departmental and corporate needs.
▸ Establishes market coverage plans and establishes good customer rapport.
▸ Provides input to corporate processes such as Product/Service forecasts, competitive intelligence, sales plans, customer records and other administrative reports.
▸ Interprets sales results and assists in the development of appropriate action plans (e.g. Wins/losses).
▸ Ensures the establishment and execution of high quality account plans that affect business expansion opportunities, fortification of client relationships, and ensure client satisfaction.

Other
▸ Be aware and adhere to all applicable Health and Safety Regulations, in accordance with Legislation and related Company Policy.
▸ Makes formal group presentations as required.

Competencies
▸ Qualifications Core Competencies: Customer Service Orientation, Initiative, Teamwork and Collaboration
▸ Role Specific Competencies: Business Acumen, Team Leadership, Problem Solving

▸ Minimum of 5 years sales experience and a University Degree in Commerce, Business Administration majoring in sales/marketing or an equivalent combination of education and work experience preferred.

Behaviours
▸ Previous experience in developing a professional and effective sales approach
▸ Ability to communicate and maintain superior business relationships with a range of clients.
▸ Ability to work with minimum direction/supervision to meet business objectives.
▸ Ability to lead and motivate others to achieve aggressive goals in managing partner relationships.

Step 2: *Next, match the behaviours to the competencies and list potential behavioural questions that could be asked to assess these competencies:*

Competencies and Respective Behaviours	Potential Questions
Customer Service Orientation ▸ Establishes rapport with key customer influencers and decision makers ▸ Establishes market coverage plans and establishes good customer rapport. ▸ Ability to communicate and maintain superior business relationships with a range of clients	Tell me about a time you had to build good rapport with a customer who was difficult to work with
Initiative ▸ Initiates intensive prospecting of the existing customer base to generate new customer applications covering the full range of info. system/services ▸ Ability to work with minimum direction / supervision to meet business objectives	Tell me about a time you were able to reach stretch sale targets
Teamwork and Collaboration ▸ Ability to lead and motivate others to achieve aggressive goals in managing partner relationships.	Tell me about a time where your team failed to reach a goal
Business Acumen ▸ Conducts needs analysis to determine departmental and Corporate needs ▸ Provides input to Corporate processes such as Product/Service forecasts, competitive intelligence, sales plans, customer records and other administrative reports	Tell me about a time you motivated your team members to achieve a goal that was considered impossible or very difficult
Problem Solving ▸ Develops sales strategies and obtain established sales objectives ▸ Overcomes roadblocks in the decision-making process and closes at appropriate levels ▸ Interprets sales results and assists in the development of appropriate action plans (e.g. Wins/losses).	Tell me about a time you had to resolve a difficult problem

Step 4: *If the job advertisement indicates a required knowledge or task, put these items in the "Other" category. Be prepared to provide an example where you applied this knowledge or performed a similar task. For example,*

Other	Make Sure I...
Makes formal group presentations as required	Talk about the presentation I gave to a new start up company where I had to facilitate a change in agenda on the spot
Be aware and adhere to all applicable Health and Safety Regulations, in accordance with Legislation and related Company Policy	Use the example about the time I was asked to prepare a report that required research on this legislation.

 # JOB ADVERTISMENT TIP

Whether you match the behaviours accurately to the competency does not matter as much; what's important is that you provide examples that demonstrate the behaviours important to the job.

▶ Mistake #2: Not preparing multiple examples per question

Many organizations will bring you back for a 2nd, 3rd, 4th or even a 5th interview to ask you questions similar to those they asked before. They do this purposefully to get you to give different examples that would demonstrate you are consistent in your behaviours. If you freeze up or give the exact same response each time, they may wonder if you are only a "one hit wonder"

Strategy: Have Two Examples for Each Competency Required for the Job

Two?!?!!, "It's hard enough coming up with one!", "Isn't this over-preparing?" Those are probably some of the thoughts running though your mind. Well, think about it this way: What would you do if the interviewer asked, "Can you give me another example?"

If you give an answer and for some reason the interviewer doesn't find it satisfactory he may ask you for another example.

You could use an example that you had already talked about in answer to a previous question if you're highlighting a different point. For example, maybe you were the Editor of the school newspaper. You would probably use this example to highlight your leadership skills. You could probably use this example to talk about your team building skills as well. These two competencies have different descriptions, so when you discuss them, you could be citing different situations relating to the same experience.

You could also prepare a variety of different examples taken from school, work, extra-curricular activities, volunteer experiences, or sports teams to demonstrate that you are well-rounded. Jot your notes in point form, using key words to help you remember what you want to highlight. Structure your notes in the BAR format so you could remember it in that order. We have an example of a Behavioural Examples worksheet (see Appendix section) that you could use to help you prepare for at least two examples per competency. When you finish preparing your notes, practice delivering your answers out loud!

▶ Mistake #3: Not Knowing Why You Are Applying

"Well, I am looking to get my foot in the door of any company" or
"My internet was down so I did not get a chance to research your website."
This is not convincing. How you came to select a company to work for is
important. Most interviewers will ask you why you applied for the job and
what you know about the organization. If you tell an interviewer that you
haven't researched the organization, it demonstrates that you don't care
about where you work, which could be translated into you don't care about
doing a good job.

Strategy: Research the Organization and the Hiring Process

Learn as much as you can prior to the interview about the organization and the
hiring process. Reading and extracting from the job ad is a good start but you
need to do more if you want to stand out from the crowd! Doing research will
help you:

- ▶ Ask the interviewer insightful questions
- ▶ Show that you are sincerely interested in the organization
- ▶ Know what to expect throughout the recruitment process

▶ INTERVIEW TIP

*Since you will likely only be asked one question
to test your knowledge of the organization,
"what do you know/like about us?" don't
spend too much time doing this research.
Aim to have some knowledge rather than
no knowledge at all.*

Information you should seek:

Company Related

- ▸ company reputation
- ▸ internal professional development, training and career paths
- ▸ employee benefits
- ▸ structures, divisions, affiliates and subsidiaries
- ▸ type of company, locations, number of employees
- ▸ profits, revenues and sales
- ▸ competitors within the industry
- ▸ past history and future growth potential

Recruitment Related

- ▸ hiring process
- ▸ competencies they are looking for and what they mean to that organization?
- ▸ any other qualities they are looking for
- ▸ perspective on direct work-related experience
- ▸ importance of extra-curricular activities
- ▸ how your responses will be assessed

Sources to get information may include:

- ▸ public sources
- ▸ company web site
- ▸ independent information sites
- ▸ unofficial or official company guides
- ▸ annual report
- ▸ at school
- ▸ posted job description
- ▸ career centers
- ▸ career fairs
- ▸ information sessions
- ▸ networks
- ▸ the interviewer
- ▸ people you know who had previously applied to or interviewed with that organization

▶ Mistake #4: Not having fun at the interview

Some candidates succeed in putting interviewers to sleep because they do not exhibit energy. Other candidates look scared and appear as if they are undergoing torture! Enthusiasm is infectious and is essential to keeping the interviewer interested in you. You do not have to be an energizer bunny but you do need to demonstrate passion for what you want to do. Passion will give you the fuel to do the job well. You need to appear as if you are enjoying the interview.

Strategy: Psych Yourself Out!

You've heard the numerous clichés: "It's all in the mind", "Confidence goes a long way", etc. And it's true! Before you go to your interview make sure you are in a great frame of mind. Chemically, how your body feels can also have an affect. It's important you're thinking positive thoughts about yourself and your body feels pumped. Here are some tips on how to do that:

- ▸ Drink coffee or have a chocolate bar. Either or both could increase your ability to think on your feet or give you a good kick for the first hour.
- ▸ Talk to yourself! Tell yourself that YOU are awesome! Quickly run through your mind 5 things that you're proud of and why you're proud of them.
- ▸ SMILE! Keep it glued on your face for a while, the way your face is set naturally affects the way your brain thinks and the way your heart and body feels
- ▸ Laugh! Think of something funny and laugh/chuckle/giggle about it. Laughter will make you feel good
- ▸ Get your mind off of the interview. Listen to the radio, read a book or magazine/newspaper article. Getting your mind on things other than the interview can help you be natural when it starts.
- ▸ Take several DEEP breaths! Your heart rate may be racing and deep breathing will help slow it down and stop you from sweating!

▶ Mistake #5: Not preparing for small talk

The time between saying "hi" in the lobby and taking the elevator up to the interview room or walking down the corridor could be the longest time before the interview! Some candidates make the mistake of not talking during this period or if they do talk, they talk about things that do not help the interviewer like them. For example, one candidate was asked the question, "how was your weekend?" She gave a long description of what she did with her boyfriend and how they almost broke up. As a quick tip, please do not talk about very personal experiences during the small talk and definitely do not talk about it during the interview.

Strategy: Make the First 30 Seconds Count

Some people believe that an interviewer makes up his mind in the first 30 seconds of the interview. Scary, huh? Well, if that is true you probably don't want your fate decided for you before you get a chance to prove yourself. Let's make sure you score well here!

Many of the tips are very common sense, but this quick check list of **DO's** and **DON'Ts** can help you make the first 30 seconds count in your favour.

DO's:

1. Present a warm, friendly & welcoming aura (smile!); sometimes, the interviewer is pretty nervous too!

2. If you are sitting, STAND UP to shake the interviewer's hand

3. Engage in small talk on your way to the interviewing room. You could talk about...
    - something interesting you did over the weekend
    - front page news items are safe (not about politics, religion or a terrible crime)
    - something the interviewer will likely relate to (an upcoming holiday etc)

4. Make your small talk sound spontaneous and not rehearsed

5. Make a joke if the occasion presents itself but don't strive to find a joke. A common initiated topic from the interviewer would be about whether the place was "easy to find". If you have a funny incident on your way to the interview talk about it.

DON'Ts:

1. Be stiff/curt "professional"

2. Discuss the weather. It's obvious you have nothing else to say

3. Initiate discussions about the job or company. This may be a signal that you are nervous or can't handle talking about other things. Besides, there will be lots of time during the actual interview to talk about these things.

4. Be uncomfortable with silence, this may show that you are nervous.

5. Be afraid to accept a beverage (at least water) if it's offered to you and you see it's readily available. This shows you are confident.

▶ Mistake #6:
Not knowing how to summarize key strengths

Some candidates make the mistake of providing a never ending list of reasons why they should be hired. They talk about their job history and then boost about how good they are. There is no need to restate your job history; it is on your résumé. Secondly, let the interviewer determine how good you are because that is his job.

Strategy: Have a One Minute Pitch

At the beginning of the interview, an interviewer may ask *"Tell me something about yourself?"* or at the conclusion of the interview, you may be asked *"Tell us why we should hire you?"* These questions help the interviewer assess your ability to summarize key points. Your response needs to have impact and this could be the defining moment that will convince the interviewer that you are the right person for the job.

"Tell me something about yourself?" is a generic question and allows you the opportunity to say whatever you want. The interviewer wants to get a first impression of you. This question is usually used as an interview icebreaker. One way of answering this question is to refer to both personal traits and competencies the job requires. Refer to the Well-Roundedness and Attitude sections of the Holistic Q&A chapter. Don't waste this opportunity to impress by telling the interviewer a bunch of things that do absolutely nothing for you. For example, telling the interviewer you like animals and have several pets is irrelevant unless you were applying to work with animals.

"Tell us why we should hire you?" is a more specific question, and the interviewer is telling you he wants you to specifically address his core competency needs. If you've done your homework, then you should know what these needs are. Refer to the *Using the Job Ad to Anticipate Questions and remember to use BAR.*

To prepare for the one minute pitch, do the following:
1. Understand the top three competencies required to do the job well.
2. Understand your top three competencies that match the requirements of the job
3. Briefly describe how you have in the past or could in the future help the organization move forward

Here is an example of a 1 Minute Pitch (we will assume this interview is for the job ad you saw earlier in the Using the Job Ad to Anticipate Questions section:

"Tell us why we should hire you."

Necessary Competencies	Addressing the Competency
▸ Initiates intensive prospecting of the existing customer base to generate new customers ▸ Establishes good customer rapport ▸ Establish and executes high quality account plans that will expand the business	**B** From what you have told me, it sounds like your organization has two priorities: to restore previously poorly serviced accounts and to establish new accounts. I have confidence I could take on this challenge. **A** As this year's Athletic Director of the Commerce Students Association, I needed to increase participation in our intramural league. In previous years, only 5% of Commerce students participated. I felt it was important to better understand student needs, so I initiated 1:1 discussions and group discussions. I made sure I understood the needs of students who did participate, as well as those who did not. **R** In the end, I came up with events that targeted unmet needs, such as rock-climbing where students were not intimidated by the expertise of others as most students didn't know how to climb, and a beach event so that students could participate together but still have choices in what they wanted to do (frisbee, volleyball, rollerblade, etc). I tripled participation levels and we are now getting unsolicited feedback on other events students want us to organize! I am confident that I could use these same skills to bring about the strong revival needs for your department.

▶ Mistake #7: Not preparing to say why you are not good

Some candidates provide wonderful examples of how they performed well in a situation but when they are asked to describe a situation where they failed, they can not find an example. When asked about a weakness or mistake they made, some candidates may try to side-step the question by giving a trivial or vague answer. While this may reduce the amount of negative information given to the interviewer, it may also cause the interviewer to think that you are not honest, may have something to hide, or don't have the skills to handle a difficult situation.

No one is perfect and it is understandable that we all make mistakes. Thinking about when you made a mistake and what you would do differently is important.

Strategy: Bring Negatives to Positives

Questions that ask you to reveal something negative about yourself is inevitable and can make you uncomfortable, here are six (6) tips on how to overcome that.

 **Tip**

Use BAR:

When you are trying to sound like the best candidate for a job and you suddenly have to tell why that may not be the case, your mind gets caught off guard and you may stumble for an answer. You may forget the techniques you've been taught. Don't. **BAR** is a powerful technique and can help you deliver a strong answer.

Tip

Show improvement:

Use past tense. Indicate what you have learned and how your results are now better than before. However, don't say how long ago the mistake was made because then you may be prompted for a current problem. Indicate that it is something you have been working on, and are still doing today, but that you've found a way to improve. Instead of focusing on the obstacle, focus on how you overcame it!

Tip

Give a meaningful answer:

If the interviewer asks you to reveal something negative about yourself, chances are, he's asking other candidates to do the same thing. It is an opportunity to place yourself ahead of others, so don't be afraid of it and throw the chance away by giving a trivial or vague answer. For example, if the question asks for a mistake you've made, don't give an example where the mistake is common human error like, *"I had to do a lot of data entry for a summer job, and sometimes I entered the data wrong. I learned to double check my entries and stopped making those errors."* This does not give the interviewer insight about your fit for the job. Sometimes these answers even cause scepticism because they may sound like you are hiding something or have no insight into your own weaknesses.

Another common bad answer revolves around taking on too much work. You may be trying to sound like a hard worker, but these answers can cause several negative thoughts: you can't finish your work, you finish your work but the quality is not good, you may not pull your weight, it takes you a long time to learn new things, etc. Vague answers usually prompt the interviewer to ask follow up questions so make sure you have an answer ready. For example, if the question asks why you left a previous job, and your answer is, *"I wanted a bigger challenge"* or *"I wanted a change"*, the interviewer may ask, *"Why?"* or *"What did you mean by that?"*

 **Tip**

Apply your competency/holistic knowledge:

You may have noticed you've already seen a few of these questions in previous competency/holistic examples. That is because the interviewer's goal has not changed — he is assessing your fit for the job. Use this fact to your advantage. Never use an important competency as one of your weaknesses instead, slide it in as a strength! If you've done your research, you would know which competencies are important to the interviewer. For example, if the question is "Where do you think you need improvement?" and you know that creativity and initiative is important, a good answer may sound like this:

"I am usually very creative with new ideas on how to build the business, and I usually take the initiative to get things started. This has brought about some good results, but sometimes my excitement to try something new has caused difficulties because I'm proposing change. However, I don't think I should hold back on being creative or taking initiative. I think where I need to improve is my presentation skills for communicating change. I need to better understand others' fears and concerns so that I can alleviate them when I'm making proposals. Current results may be good, and I need to ensure people's efforts are recognized. Instead of sounding like I'm proposing something different, I need to position it as how to make the situation better. I've been trying to remember this, and when I do, I've noticed that people are more receptive."

Not only have you reinforced your creativity and initiative skills, you've also highlighted your improvement in communication as well as your problem solving skills!

 **Tip**

Don't talk about relationship problems if there was no resolution:

Disagreement examples are good if they have positive outcomes. However, disagreements or conflicts with others that are unresolved may leave the interviewer wondering if you are difficult to work with. Even if you could make your side sound reasonable, the interviewer will wonder about perspective from the others' points of view. People conflicts should always be avoided if the outcome was negative; otherwise it makes the interviewer sceptical about you.

 **Tip**

Keep it short:

There's no need to dwell here, the longer your answer, the more if feels like you are justifying your actions. Instead, spend more time on answers that focus on your strengths.

▶ Mistake #8:
Not preparing to answer technical questions for a non-technical position

To be clear, if you are interviewing for a technical position this book can definitely help you with some aspects of the job. However, we would still strongly advise you to seek additional help to answer specific technical questions. Some candidates make the mistake of thinking that since they are not interviewing for a job such as a computer programmer, they don't need to worry about technical questions. This may be true most of the time, but sometimes, the interviewer just wants to get a feel for how much training you'd need to use simple everyday tools.

Strategy: Prepare to answer a technical question in BAR format to Holistic Questions

Interviewers may ask you about your knowledge of a subject or experience in a particular area to assess whether you have the necessary technical skills to perform the job. For new graduates with limited work experience, technical questions may be focused on coursework. For example, do you know the key elements for financial reporting, specifics about programming language or how to create a marketing plan? When technical questions are asked, the interviewer is looking to determine whether you…

- ▶ Possess necessary technical skills to effectively do the job
- ▶ Would require additional training than what they currently offer
- ▶ Could be a resource and teach others specific tools

When you answer technical questions, remember to use **BAR**. Provide actual examples of when you've used the tools/programs and highlight something you've achieved or created because of a specific tool or program. For example, if you were asked "How well do you know how to use this computer program?" you could say:

> **B** I know it pretty well because I use it regularly as part of my course work.
> **A** For example, for a recent project, I had to create models and flow charts with it, as well as activate animation. I can create slide show presentations, insert files from other sources, convert them to and from other applications, etc.
> **R** I've delivered presentations using this tool which helped make them more interesting and fun to watch.

▶ Mistake #9: Not knowing what to ask the interviewer

Interviews are a two way process. The interviewer will ask questions to see if you are the right person for the job and in return you should ask the interviewer questions to see if this is the right job and organization for you! Candidates who do not ask questions in an interview signal that they are really not that interested. On the other hand, if candidates ask questions that could be easily researched in advance, this may imply that they do not take initiative. This may leave you wondering which questions you should ask and which questions you shouldn't ask! Here's what to do:

Strategy: Create categories to help you come up with questions

Being curious is all about asking insightful questions. It is about truly making the interview a two-way exchange of information. More importantly it is to help you identify whether this organization is one where you really want to work for. ALWAYS ask questions at the end of the interview to reinforce your interest in the job and to find out if this is the job for you. Try not to ask basic questions that can be answered by visiting the company website. Sometimes, if a candidate provides satisfactory responses but concluded the interview with insightful questions, this may sway the interviewers to consider giving the candidate a second chance. Although, this part of your interview may not count for a lot, the types of questions you ask may be your saving grace. To demonstrate you thought carefully about the job, ask for clarification on areas of interest or areas where you have researched. At the end of the interview, don't forget to ask about the next steps in the recruiting process and when you expect to hear from the interviewer. Some examples of questions you could ask are:

Questions to determine if this organization is for you

  ▸ If you could change one thing about working for _____, what would that be?

  ▸ How many new hires stay with the company for 5 or more years?

  ▸ Describe the culture in the organization. In your department.

- Does the organization have plans to expand internationally?

- Could you tell me which new markets the organization is currently considering entering?

- I am interested in learning more about _____as mentioned in the _____?

- What do you like best and least about your job and/or the organization?

Questions to determine if the position is for you

- What type of assignment can I expect in the first year?

- What made the previous person in this job successful?

- How much travel is required in this job?

- How many projects does a person work on simultaneously?

- What are the immediate and longer term issues that you will require the person in _____to address?

- Where do opportunities for improvement exist in this job?

- What is your long term vision for your department (or the organization)?

- To achieve the long term goals you just spoke about, how do you see this position evolve/how do you see the person in this position fit in?

- Where does this position fit in the overall organizational structure?

- Who was in the position before, and where are they now?

- How long did the individual stay in the position?

Questions to determine if you will get along with your manager

▸ How often will performance be evaluated?

▸ How would you describe your team?

▸ What is it like to work in your team?

▸ What are your expectations?

▸ What is one thing your employees do that bug you?

▸ How would you describe your management style?

▸ How is this department structured?

▸ What has been the impact of restructuring on this department?

▸ What is the most pressing issue faced by your department?

Questions to determine if the position will help you grow

▸ What type of career paths may be taken by those who begin as _____?

▸ Could you tell me more about the training program for new hires?

▸ What type of support networks exist for new hires?

▸ How does the organization identify and retain high performers?

▸ How long does it usually take to get to the next couple of levels?

▸ How is performance measured/evaluated?

▸ Can you give me an example of how an exceptional new hire has performed?

▶ Mistake #10:
Not knowing you got the wrong reference!

Some candidates may do very well in an interview but then make the mistake of providing an inappropriate reference (someone who can't answer the relevant reference check questions) or a bad reference (someone who says negative things about you). A bad or inappropriate reference may cost the candidate the job.

Strategy: Getting the Right Strong References

Getting the right person to vouch for you is important. References can either give you that extra edge over another candidate or it could eliminate you from consideration. You need to be careful in your choices. Even if someone is willing to give you a reference, it doesn't mean they will give a *good* reference. To line up strong references, take the following steps:

1. Identify references from 3-5 different experiences (academic, previous work experiences, and volunteer experiences, etc)

2. Reflect on whether you provided good or exceptional performance to the references selected

3. Call the reference where you felt you did a good job and ask if he/she "would feel comfortable giving you a strong reference".

4. If the answer is yes, tell your reference the company and position you've applied for

5. Send your reference a summary of some of your key accomplishments at that specific experience and a recent copy of your résumé to refresh the reference's memory.

6. Follow up with a thank you note and let your reference know if you landed the job.

▶ Mistake #11:
Not knowing how to turn a
bad interview into a good one!

When an interview is over, many candidates think that they can't do anything about it. The truth is you could learn from your interview mistakes. The biggest mistake is not reflecting on your interview performance and using this information to avoid making the same mistake at your next interview.

Strategy: Self Assess Your Interview Performance

Immediately after you leave the interview, record all the questions you were asked. This will help you obtain a library of questions for subsequent interviews with the same or different organization. The questions will also help you assess your performance. Once you get home, think about what you said and how you said it. For instance,

- ▶ Were you honest in the answers you gave? Why or why not?
- ▶ Were your responses focused and concise?
- ▶ Did you use BAR? Was your background sufficient? Were your actions impactful enough? Were your results strong enough?
- ▶ Did you use the best possible example?
- ▶ If you were to answer this question again, what would say differently?

Use the worksheet *Interview Self Assessment* to record the questions you were asked and assess your interview performance

Conclusion

Get the *INTERVIEW EDGE!*

Tips to Getting Hired from Interviewers

Conclusion

Succeeding in an interview requires knowing what the interviewer wants, having a technique to deliver a strong and consistent image and believing in yourself! This book has armed you with the knowledge you need to succeed. You now have in your hands:

▸ Information about what interviewers are looking for when they ask you behavioural and holistic questions

▸ A powerful technique to deliver strong answers: **BAR**

▸ Real examples of behavioural and holistic responses

▸ Tips on how to avoid mistakes most candidates make

However, this information alone will not win you the job. You must practice applying this knowledge by researching the job, predicting questions that you will be asked, preparing your responses to the anticipated questions and delivering your answers out loud. Practicing is key to your success as a job applicant. Practicing will give you the confidence to perform well in the interview. Practicing will ease any nervousness you may have. Practicing will make the interview more enjoyable for you. Practicing will help you present a more positive impression. Practicing will ultimately lead you to become the top 0.2% that organizations hire!

We wish you the best of luck in your search for a successful career.
If you would like any additional help, please feel free to contact us at
gethirednow@gmail.com or www.gettingyouhired.com

Appendix

Worksheets & Cheat Sheets

Worksheet for Drafting Multiple Behavioural Examples

Competency & Definition	School Example	Work Example	Extra-Curricular Example	Other Experience

 # Worksheet for Drafting BAR Answers

For each competency, recall a relevant moment and write down the key details of the background, the action you took and result.

Competency	
Possible Question(s)	**Background**
	Action
	Results

Competency	
Possible Question(s)	**Background**
	Action
	Results

▶ Cheat Sheets for Behavioural Competencies

12 Behavioural Competencies

▶ Leadership   ▶ Analytical Thinking   ▶ Communication

▶ Risk-Taking   ▶ Creative Thinking   ▶ Results-Oriented

▶ Teamwork   ▶ Ethics   ▶ Learning

▶ Time Management   ▶ Initiative   ▶ Flexibility

▶ Leadership

Recognizes opportunities and has vision to achieve them. Gains others' support for ideas and solutions and energizes them to work towards a common goal. Maximizes individual strengths and potential. Makes tough decisions.

Skill Level	Description
WEAK	▸ Has no vision; does not set directions ▸ Follows directions or prescribed instructions ▸ Participates as a member rather than leads ▸ Leads through fear ▸ Wants everyone to do things "one way"
STRONG	▸ Identifies opportunities ▸ Sets a direction for change ▸ Motivates others to take action
EXCEPTIONAL	▸ Sets a stretch vision ▸ Consistently selected by others to lead ▸ Inspires exceptional performance in others ▸ Anticipates and addresses potential obstacles ▸ Achieves exceptional results

▶ Risk-Taking

Pursues potential opportunities that may result in positive results but may lead to negative consequences. Evaluates risks by weighing pros and cons; takes action in the face of uncertainties.

Skill Level	Description
WEAK	▸ Sets easily attainable goals ▸ Delays action ▸ Acts without evaluating risks
STRONG	▸ Sets challenging goals ▸ Takes action towards goals ▸ Seeks information to minimize risks
EXCEPTIONAL	▸ Sets stretch goals ▸ Demonstrates sense of urgency ▸ Evaluates risks and makes calculated decisions ▸ Is courageous in championing initiatives despite adversity and uncertainty ▸ Applies learnings to new experiences

▸ Teamwork

Works cooperatively with diverse people to achieve common goals. Builds mutual respect and trust by listening and encouraging different points of views. Leverages individual members' strengths.

Skill Level	Description
WEAK	▸ Works competitively rather than co-operatively ▸ Prefers to work alone ▸ Does not seek out different perspectives ▸ Avoids conflict
STRONG	▸ Collaborates with others towards a common objective ▸ Values and elicits others' expertise and perspectives ▸ Respects, understands and trusts others ▸ Works to resolve conflict if present
EXCEPTIONAL	▸ Enables groups to work together rather than working in silos to achieve exceptional results ▸ Has strong influence on team outcomes without being perceived as dominant ▸ Brings out others strengths and leverages each person's area of expertise ▸ Creates an atmosphere of trust, mutual respect and open sharing ▸ Publicly recognizes others for their strong performance

▸ Time Management

Prioritizes multiple responsibilities and deadlines effectively. Eliminates wasted efforts by knowing when and how to seek others' expertise. Breaks larger assignments into manageable chunks. Re-evaluates priorities on a regular basis. Spends time working on the most significant or time-sensitive tasks first. Finds improved ways of doing things to increase efficiency.

Skill Level	Description
WEAK	▸ Has no systematic way of managing time ▸ Avoids dealing with multiple responsibilities ▸ Handles tasks one at a time ▸ Comfortable with current processes even if inefficient ▸ Avoids dealing with complexity
STRONG	▸ Prioritizes and breaks assignments into manageable chunks ▸ Co-ordinates schedules with others to meet deadlines ▸ Delegates tasks appropriately ▸ Achieves balance between personal, academic and work objectives ▸ Consistently meets deadlines ▸ Finds improved ways of getting results
EXCEPTIONAL	▸ Is pro-active in anticipating needs and demands that may interrupt schedule ▸ Deals with time constraints creatively ▸ Adopts time saving measures without impacting quality ▸ Has exceptional ability to take on new initiatives and get them done ▸ Applies the 80-20 principle ▸ Not only meets deadlines but achieves high level of performance results ▸ Encourages others to develop their skills to improve overall efficiency

▸ Analytical Thinking

Ability to think critically and breaks situation into smaller pieces to organize thoughts/process in a step-by-step approach. Analyzes data, creates alternatives and uses a logical approach to problem solving. Clearly identifies patterns in complex and unorganized data. Finds relationships between seemingly unrelated issues.

Skill Level	Description
WEAK	▸ Has difficulties sorting through complex data and identifying key issues ▸ Has experience with relatively simple problems or unable to solve complex problems ▸ Lacks systematic approach in problem solving; uses a trial and error approach ▸ Selects from a limited number of pre-established responses
STRONG	▸ Sorts through complex data and identifies relevant points ▸ Identifies sources and symptoms of problems ▸ Quickly grasps critical issues in a problem and develops solutions ▸ Analyzes data to create alternatives ▸ Usually questions assumptions ▸ Interprets data to identify possibly emerging problems
EXCEPTIONAL	▸ Does not accept information at face value but probes to understand the data ▸ Evaluates and interprets complex, controversial or obscure information, identify gaps and derives relevant meaning ▸ Proposes alternative approaches to unfamiliar situations or concepts ▸ Interprets the impact of potential solutions on external elements ▸ Creates precedent-setting solutions

▸ Creative Thinking

Curious, imaginative and thinks "outside the box". Consistently pursues innovative and new learning. Explores new or recombines knowledge to generate novel and valuable solutions. Uses intuition and looks beyond status quo to create new insights.

Skill Level	Description
WEAK	▸ Tends to be narrow in thinking or resistance to change ▸ Uncomfortable with novel ideas or approaches ▸ Follows precedent rather than generates new solutions ▸ Fear of mistakes prevents action
STRONG	▸ Has a broad view and open to change ▸ Asks "Why?" ▸ Tries new approaches to get better results ▸ Imports solutions from outside environment
EXCEPTIONAL	▸ Takes action to change perspectives or break from status quo ▸ Asks "What if?" ▸ Combines knowledge in new ways to solve old problems ▸ Generates new ideas that are not constrained by traditional views ▸ Imports and modifies solutions from outside environment ▸ Creates new theory

▸ Ethics

Consistently and without exception exhibits high standards of fairness and integrity when dealing with others. Does not jeopardize others' interests for personal benefits. Is trusted and respected by others. Does not compromise sound principles, values and standards under any circumstances.

Skill Level	Description
WEAK	▸ Aware of the importance of ethical behaviour and its impact on trust and influence ▸ Behaviours are inconsistent ▸ Sees potential conflicts of interests but just tries to minimize severity
STRONG	▸ Exemplifies high standards of honest and ethical behaviours ▸ Effectively manages conflicts of interest ▸ Avoids action or statements that compromise integrity
EXCEPTIONAL	▸ Sticks to principles even when unpopular to do so ▸ Takes responsibility for failures and mistakes without blaming others or circumstances ▸ Models and encourages ethical behaviours ▸ Earns and maintains the trust of others by acting consistently ▸ Proactive in safeguarding integrity and principles ▸ Prevents situations of conflicts of interests from coming up

▸ Initiative

Takes action without being prompted by others or with minimum direction, support or approval. Recognizes alternatives to potential problems before they become obvious.

Skill Level	Description
WEAK	▸ Carries out tasks that are expected ▸ May raise issues for improvements ▸ Understands the need to seek improvement but does not take action until request is made
STRONG	▸ Takes action to resolve problems without waiting to be asked ▸ Anticipates future needs or opportunities and proposes action plan to achieve desired results ▸ Is comfortable taking risks and challenging way things are done
EXCEPTIONAL	▸ Strives to achieve goals beyond what is required ▸ Anticipates and acts on changes, trends or emerging issues ▸ Challenges the way things are done and takes action towards improvements ▸ Proactively leads new projects; inspires and involves others to take on new initiatives ▸ Completes initiative even when it becomes difficult

▶ Communication

Presents information in a clear and concise manner. Effectively gets others to open up by actively listening, asking appropriate questions and responding appropriately. Is persuasive.

Skill Level	Description
WEAK	▸ Unable to influence others ▸ Muffled/hesitant/stammering speech ▸ Pays attention when others talk and takes notes when appropriate ▸ Does not ask questions to understand others point of view
STRONG	▸ Conveys information, ideas, thoughts and feelings in a clear and professional manner ▸ Influences others ▸ Seeks to ensure facts are clearly understood ▸ Listens actively, reads body language and subtle messages
EXCEPTIONAL	▸ Ability to persuade others and sell ideas ▸ Seeks to understand, then to be understood ▸ Understands others' underlying needs, interests, issues and motivators ▸ Catches and interprets conflicting messages or actions ▸ Adapts style, words and action depending on audience ▸ Identifies barriers to communication and takes action to facilitate mutual understanding ▸ Explains complex concepts, thoughts and ideas clearly and concisely to all levels ▸ Challenges others' ideas tactfully while managing disagreements constructively

▶ Results-Oriented

Sets ambitious goals and demonstrates resiliency in achieving them. Tracks progress in meeting objectives, set priorities and overcomes barriers to completing tasks. Has high level of commitment to start and complete projects, even in the face of adversity. Focuses on end result and not on individual styles of achieving results. Self disciplined, success oriented and has tenacity.

Skill Level	Description
WEAK	▸ Produces only what is required ▸ Explores how to deliver additional work outcomes when requested ▸ Requires direction and supervision ▸ Won't work with difficult personalities ▸ Unwilling to make sacrifices to get results
STRONG	▸ Can work with difficult personalities ▸ Accomplishes priorities through careful planning and execution ▸ Makes some sacrifices in time/plans/energy for the sake of a work objective ▸ Anticipates, recognizes and seize opportunities
EXCEPTIONAL	▸ Makes personal sacrifices in order to reach goal ▸ Has strong sense of urgency ▸ Perseveres over extended period of time to overcome significant obstacles ▸ Stretches self and others to pursue difficult but possible goals ▸ Consistently attempts to improve vs. past results ▸ Focus on solution rather than process — see barriers as something to overcome as opposed to a reason to stop

▶ Learning

Recognizes areas of personal strength and areas of development opportunity. Takes steps to build on expertise through self development and the acquisition of new knowledge.

Skill Level	Description
WEAK	▸ Views learning as a passive rather than active exercise ▸ Shows no curiosity to learn new approaches or knowledge ▸ Has acquired basic knowledge through coursework only ▸ Willing to participate in planned learning sessions ▸ Usually behind on trends ▸ Uncomfortable working in areas different from experiences
STRONG	▸ Actively pursues learning and development opportunities to achieve results and contribute to continuous improvements ▸ Reflects on performance, both successes and failures, to see how things could have been done differently for better results ▸ Proactively identifies new ways of doing things and learning plans ▸ Seeks feedback on performance and incorporates into improvement
EXCEPTIONAL	▸ Takes steps to maintain an in-depth knowledge of area of expertise ▸ Proactively seek others' ideas and perspectives and integrates learnings ▸ Pursues learning beyond current job or identified needs ▸ Anticipates future needs and proactively prepares to meet them ▸ Takes ownership of own professional development ▸ Focuses development in areas of greatest value ▸ Stays current in a demanding and changing environment ▸ Proactively develops others and coaches peers

▶ Flexibility

Is open to change and new information. Adapts behaviour and work methods in response to new information, changing conditions or unexpected obstacles. Adjusts and can work effectively within a variety of situations and with diverse individuals or groups.

Skill Level	Description
WEAK	▸ Listens to others' viewpoints but silently retains one's own ▸ Always follows procedures ▸ May be reluctant to try something new ▸ Critical of others actions and do not accept others differences
STRONG	▸ Willingly tries new things and compromises ▸ Decides what to do based on the circumstances of the situation ▸ Change own approach to adapt to others' responses while maintaining one's own needs
EXCEPTIONAL	▸ Effectively works in different environments, cultures, locations, technologies or various types of people ▸ Open to new ideas, circumstances and information ▸ Accepts others, and embraces differences ▸ Shifts focus and activities quickly in response to changing priorities, unexpected obstacles, new demands or tasks

▶ **Cheat Sheet for Types of Holistic Questions**

11 Most Common Holistic Questions

▸ Résumé	▸ Interest	▸ Hypothetical/Case Study
▸ Fit	▸ Strengths/Weaknesses	▸ Work Pattern
▸ Well Roundedness	▸ Drive	▸ Attitude
▸ Watch Outs	▸ Long Term Goals	

▸ Résumé

Some résumés tend to embellish the candidate's work experience. Knowing this, interviewers ask résumé questions to get you to elaborate or clarify items on your résumé to determine if you really did what you said you did. When résumé questions are asked, the interviewer is looking to...

- ▸ Validate your résumé
- ▸ Gain insight into strong competency skills
- ▸ Gain insight into indicated areas of interest

▸ Fit

How you will fit in with the company's culture, your personality and how you will get along with your team and manager are important to the interviewer. The interviewer is trying to learn more about you beyond the skills you possess. When fit questions are asked, the interviewer is looking to determine whether...

- ▸ You will thrive in the company's corporate culture
- ▸ You have similar principles and values as the company
- ▸ Your style of work and underlying motivation match the company incentives

▸ Well Roundedness

Many interviewers also look for strong extra-curricular involvement or interests outside of work and academic. These experiences not only highlight certain competencies, they demonstrate that you are someone who enjoys life. A well-rounded individual may also be perceived as someone able to help enhance the company atmosphere. These types of questions also lighten the mood and provide interesting insights into your character. When well roundness questions are asked, the interviewer is looking to determine whether...

- ▸ You can balance a heavy workload and personal life
- ▸ Your involvement in the community/volunteer work is real and not solely for display on your résumé
- ▸ You have interests outside of school/work

▸ Watch-Outs

In addition to finding reasons to hire you, interviewers also try to find reasons why they should not hire you. Watch out questions are designed to find out negative aspects about you or information that would not make you an ideal fit for the job. They highlight red flags. Interviewers are on the look out for negative patterns in your work history. When watch out questions are asked, the interviewer is looking to determine whether you...

- ▸ Have been fired before and why
- ▸ Work well with others and get along well with your past bosses
- ▸ Have bad work habits
- ▸ Can be promoted

▸ Interest

Interest refers to interest in the organization or role. Interviewers ask what you know about the organization to gage your interest level in the organization or position. Sometimes, interviewers may also be assessing where their company stacks up against other companies you have applied to. Interviewers are also afraid you may leave the company soon after being hired. They spend thousands on recruiting and training so they want to make sure they are hiring someone who will stay. When company interest questions are asked, the interviewer is looking to determine whether you…

> ▸ Are proactive in researching the company in advance
> ▸ Agree with the company's mission and values
> ▸ Have a sincere interest for the company

▸ Strengths/Weaknesses

Strength/Weakness questions help the interviewer determine how you view yourself. Your response provides insights on your ability to be reflective. It also helps the interviewer determine if you are modest or boastful. When strength/weakness questions are asked, the interviewer is looking to determine whether…

> ▸ Your weaknesses will inhibit you from succeeding in the position
> ▸ Your strengths will lead you to succeed in the position
> ▸ You are realistic in your self-assessment

▸ Drive

Your underlying motivation to succeed is important to an interviewer because it is assumed that if you want to personally do well, you will also likely help the organization progress. Interviewers are usually looking for people who will do more than just what is minimally required. When questions about your drive are asked, the interviewer is looking to determine whether you…

> ▸ Are self-motivated and want to succeed
> ▸ Would set stretch targets
> ▸ Have a positively competitive mind-set
> ▸ Desire career advancement

▸ Long Term Goals

Interviewers want to know your long term goals to determine if the job you are applying for is a step towards this future! If it is not, you would likely under perform in the job and/or leave. Your departure will cost the organization additional time and money to recruit and train. Interviewers are looking out for their best interest if they consider yours as well. When questions about your long-term goals are asked, the interviewer is determining whether…

> ▸ You have realistic long term goals
> ▸ The position is aligned with where you can and want to progress with the company
> ▸ You will or will not leave the company soon after being hired

▶ Hypothetical/Case Study

Hypothetical or case study questions help the interviewer determine how you think and how you would react and act in unfamiliar situations. The hypothetical or case study questions could be difficult because of people's natural tendency to jump into the action, without thinking about the situation in its entirety. To avoid this, listen first, summarize the case given and ask for clarification. When hypothetical or case study questions are asked, the interviewer is looking to determine whether you...

- ▸ Could think quickly
- ▸ Could perform well in unfamiliar situations
- ▸ Possess logic and reasoning
- ▸ Could handle pressure

▶ Work Pattern

Your work habits determine if the work assigned will get done. Being hard working is a good trait to have because this is interpreted to mean you will be accountable for what you do. When work pattern questions are asked, the interviewer is looking to determine whether you...

- ▸ Consistently meet deadlines
- ▸ Are reliable
- ▸ Would do what it takes to get the work done

▶ Attitude

Having a positive attitude is important to fostering a good and healthy workplace environment. Positive attitudes strengthen team relationships and leads to greater work productivity; in contrast, negative attitudes make the workplace undesirable and stressful. When attitude questions are asked, the interviewer is looking to determine whether you...

- ▸ Would contribute to a positive work environment
- ▸ Would persevere even in stressful situations
- ▸ Are willing to share and help others

▸ Interview Self Assessment

Complete the self- assessment questionnaire for each interview you attended within 2 hours of the interview. Attach the job posting, job description, your interview notes, sample responses and any other information you gathered prior or during the interview to this form.

Organization: _____ Job Applied for:_____

Name and Job Titles of Interviewers: _____

_____

Interview: ☐ 1st   ☐ 2nd   ☐ 3rd   ☐ 4th   ☐ 5th   ☐ 6th

Complete the following table by listing all the questions that were asked during the interview. Reflect on your responses and rate how you felt you did when answering these questions.

List Questions Asked	Exceptional / Very Strong	Strong	Satisfactory	Weak	Comments	What would you have done differently?

Date that thank you letter/email sent on:
  *Yes, date sent:*_____

*Indicate the date when you will follow-up on this interview. Recommended time is a minimum of one week:*_____

What was the outcome of interview?

   ☐ *Hired*   ☐ *Next interview*   ☐ *Rejected*

What was the feedback you received?

Authors

▸ *Kim Chung*

Kim has a Masters of Industrial Relations (MIR), specializing in Human Resources Management from the University of Toronto. She currently works as a Human Resources Consultant for a large non-profit organization where she has interviewed hundreds of job applicants. Kim has organized and participated in career fairs, facilitated resume and interview workshops, and coached individuals to land the job they want. During her academic studies, Kim has also spearheaded the start up of a Volunteer Consulting Program and Skills and Knowledge Exchange Program to help enhance students' competitiveness in the job market.

▸ *Elisa Hui*

Elisa is a Category Account Executive in the Market Strategy & Planning department of a global leader in the consumer packaged goods industry where she has been recognized as being amongst the top two percent of high-performance employees. She has been on their recruiting team for the last four years where she represented the company on campus at career fairs, information seminars, screened resumes and conducted interviews. Elisa has also helped numerous other people with 1:1 resume reviews, information interviews and practice interviews. She gladly puts her skills to work for you in hopes that you will find a rewarding career.

Elisa is a Mentor on Bouge, a non-profit organization which develops the next generation of leaders for Canada's knowledge economy. She also served on the Board of Directors at the Second Base Youth Shelter in Scarborough from 2001 to 2004. Elisa graduated with distinction from the University of Toronto Commerce Program where she was the Founding President of the University of Toronto Consulting Association.

www.ingramcontent.com/pod-product-compliance
Lightning Source LLC
Chambersburg PA
CBHW082036290526
45791CB00015B/2271